Lincolnshire
COUNTY COUNCIL

COMMUNITIES, CULTURAL SERVICES and ADULT EDUCATION

This book should be returned on or before the last date shown below.

NE4

To renew or order library books please telephone 01522 782010
or visit www.lincolnshire.gov.uk
You will require a Personal Identification Number.
Ask any member of staff for this.

0.

D0801105

personal
finances

How to make your money work for your life

Margaret Corridan

Prentice Hall
is an imprint of

Harlow, England • London • New York • Boston • San Francisco • Toronto • Sydney • Singapore • Hong Kong
Tokyo • Seoul • Taipei • New Delhi • Cape Town • Madrid • Mexico City • Amsterdam • Munich • Paris • Milan

PEARSON EDUCATION LIMITED

Edinburgh Gate
Harlow CM20 2JE
Tel: +44 (0)1279 623623
Fax: +44 (0)1279 431059
Website: www.pearsoned.co.uk

First published in Great Britain in 2010

© Pearson Education 2010

The right of Margaret Corridan to be identified as author of this work has been asserted by her in accordance with the Copyright, Designs and Patents Act 1988.

Pearson Education is not responsible for the content of third party internet sites.

ISBN: 978-0-273-73194-8

British Library Cataloguing-in-Publication Data
A catalogue record for this book is available from the British Library

Library of Congress Cataloging-in-Publication Data
Corridan, Margaret.
  Brilliant personal finances : how to make your money work for your life / Margaret Corridan.
    p. cm.
  Includes index.
  ISBN 978-0-273-73194-8 (pbk.)
  1. Finance, Personal. I. Title.
  HG179.C684 2010
  332.024–dc22
                                    2010006007

10 9 8 7 6 5 4 3 2 1
14 13 12 11 10

Typeset in 10/14pt Plantin by 3
Printed and bound in Great Britain by Henry Ling Ltd, Dorchester

The publisher's policy is to use paper manufactured from sustainable forests.

To Mum and Dad for providing a positive and common-sense environment while I was growing up, and to Ken, my partner, for being the one who showed me that spending my way through life is not always the way to get what you want.

Contents

About the author

Margaret Corridan is not a naturally organised person. Like most people, she has been through periods in her life when managing money was not a priority. In her 20s she was fortunate to have a well-paid job, but spent every penny – and more – on having a good time. When she hit 30 she met her partner and settled down. He was the extreme opposite in terms of his attitude to risk when managing personal finances. Her change in life priorities took Margaret from being unable to meet her overdraft and having high balances on her credit cards to developing a more healthy and balanced attitude to money management – using money to work towards her goals. It is this process that has helped her connect with people and understand the principles of managing personal finances.

Margaret started life as an electronic testing engineer working on Ministry of Defence projects, but a career change took her into accountancy. She is now a Chartered Management Accountant. She spent 13 years working in various management and financial roles within the Coca-Cola organisation supporting non financial managers in their financial decisions. In late 2007 Margaret felt there was a need for taking the principles of commonsense money management from the business world into the world of personal finance. She now runs her own accountancy practice and training business, developing bespoke training programmes and course material to meet the needs of specific organisations.

Her workshops are actively sought out as programmes for both support staff and management, and her training business is also accredited to deliver a BCS Level 2 qualification in Personal Finance.

Margaret achieved her Certificate in Education, teaching adults, at the University of Greenwich. She has also been featured on BBC Radio Berkshire discussing her principles on money management.

In her spare time Margaret grows her own food, spends time with her family and loves to dance.

Acknowledgements

Many people have contributed to this book, a lot of them well before the idea for the book was formed. Some will recognise themselves as part of the case study examples.

Specifically I would like to thank the following: all those who have attended my workshops and have helped shape the step-by-step nature of the book; Karen, my assistant, for being a commonsense sounding board when choosing the relevant tables and tools for the book; Ken, my partner, for looking after me while I spent extra time working to make time for writing. Finally, thanks to Christopher Cudmore at Pearson for his guidance and patience with me as a first-time author.

Foreword

The publication of this book is timely. When asked to write the forward, I was both pleased and honoured.

Having spent 25 years in branch banking and a further 15 helping people start businesses, it has been evident to me that very few people know how to budget and manage their own finances. We have just finished a 16-year period of growth and inflated salaries; this has hidden poor personal financial management. Now we face a time of reduced budgets and unemployment which a large proportion of the population will struggle to handle.

It is extremely frightening how little we prepare children to handle their finances in adulthood. In a must-have society, it is not surprising that we have the highest ever level of debt whilst the time bomb is still ticking on retirement where the majority of the population have no pension plans. *Brilliant Personal Finances* attempts to educate people in what to do and who to seek advice from, remembering that advisers are not specialists in all areas.

Working through this book will not be a magic wand to financial woes. It will, however, start the reader to practise discipline and financial management now. They will be enlightened to some of the mysteries of the financial world whilst encouraging people to seek advice from qualified sources to enable them to plan for the future.

Colin Willman
Chairman – Education, Skills and Business Support Policy Unit,
Federation of Small Businesses

CHAPTER 1

A good read – and a useful tool!

To accomplish great things, we must not only act, but also dream: not only plan, but also believe.

Anatole France, French writer and Nobel Prize winner

Have you ever thought, 'I wish I could be more organised with my finances' or 'Why is it I never have any money to save' or just 'Am I making the right financial decisions for my life'?

Brilliant Personal Finances will show you that you don't need to be a great mathematician or finance guru to develop money management habits that help you get the most out of the money you receive.

Maybe you have felt like one of the people in the case studies below.

Peter is tired: it is 2.00 in the morning and he never seems to be able to get to sleep these days. He has a good job, a lovely wife, Helen, a new house and car and a wardrobe full of nice clothes. Their home is furnished tastefully in a way their friends would approve of. They appear to have the perfect lifestyle, so why can't he sleep? Did it have something to do with the fact that they want to start a family, and with a constant overdraft and high credit and store card balances Peter can't see how they can manage. How is he going to tell his wife they can't really afford to have a baby?

▶

Suzanne is celebrating another birthday with her friends and family – another year gone by and no closer to her dream of travelling and seeing the world. Every year she makes the same vow: one day she will take some time out and experience a new and exciting part of the world. It seems that 'one day' will never come. There never seems to be enough money left each month to save properly. She wonders if the only way she will be able to travel will be if she wins the lottery ... but then she thinks, don't you have to buy a ticket to win?

Rob and **Andrew** are having coffee. They have been best friends since starting senior school together. Recently they completed their degrees, took two months off, then started work. They agree, it is impossible to go back to living at home with their parents and now they are actually earning money they want to make the most of it. The problem is they were never good at maths at school – they are more the creative types. So thinking about money gives them a bit of a panic attack. Rob heard that they could get a bank account each and a credit card and borrow money to get them started in a flat of their own. But Andrew's parents always said you should save before you spend, have a pension for your old age and never be in debt, so Andrew is not too sure about Rob's ideas on managing money.

Peter, Suzanne, Rob and Andrew all want to change something but don't know where to start. Add your story to the list and compare notes as we follow them through each stage of the book.

How to get what you need most from this book

This book is your own *personal finance workshop*: one that you can complete at your own pace. It is not a get-rich-quick book. You can, if you wish, spend a good plane-journey amount of time, reading through each chapter and taking the principles from the book to form a plan of action when you get back home. A few tips:

- Use the book with a pencil in hand. The tasks are an important part of the journey and without them you may not end up where you want to be.
- Use it on your own, or share the tasks with the other people in your household. If you have shared financial responsibilities then it makes sense for everyone in the household to get involved, even the children.
- Use the tips, tools and principles that match with your circumstances. If you do not have children then some of the tips involving the family will not be appropriate. Take the ones that are relevant and use them every day.
- Use this book as a reference for some of the jargon-busting definitions.
- Use this book along with the popular money-saving and comparison websites to bring your action plan to reality.
- Make sure you work through Chapter 2 before you look at anything else. It is the foundation for being brilliant with personal finances.

What you will find in the book

The chapters are a logical step-by-step guide to becoming more confident with your personal finances. All the steps are equally valid – whether or not you are in a mess financially, or feel quite organised and just want to improve going forward.

The journey begins with you discovering your reason or reward for improving the way you manage your personal finances. You will then move on to using tools that help you understand your current financial state. With both of these areas covered, you can use the exercise results to look at your options, plan a route and take action.

The journey never ends. From now on, when you get close to achieving your goal or reward, you then get to choose another one and continue on your way (see Figure 1.1).

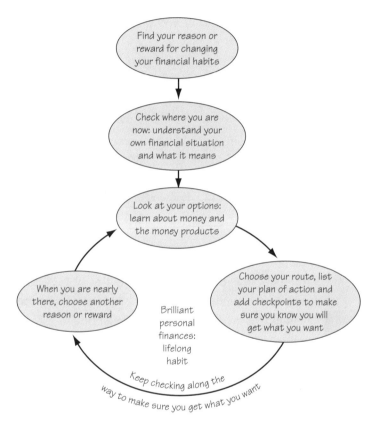

Figure 1.1 Brilliant personal finances: your personal journey

This journey is reflected in the chapters of the book as follows.

Chapter 2 – Finding the motivation and reward

This is the most important chapter in the book. Do not try and change your money management habits without reading this chapter. It will help you find the key to making decisions and the motivation to make lifestyle changes. This chapter includes thinking time and templates for you to record your thoughts. The tasks in this chapter will help you determine the key rewards you are aiming for and how they must impact your approach to managing personal finances.

Chapter 3 – Your money personality and why it is important

This chapter will help you understand why the best financial intentions often don't result in brilliant personal finances. The chapter encourages you to think about which money products you should consider or which you should avoid, and explains how to protect yourself from your money personality.

Chapter 4 – Discovering the state of your finances

This is the first chapter in the book that helps you to look at the current state of your finances. This chapter challenges you to a 10-minute review of your income and spending, revealing how in control you think you are. The chapter gives you a simple template that will help you decide whether or not your current habits are helping you reach your goals.

Chapter 5 – Understanding your credit score and how to influence it

This chapter explains credit reports and credit scores and why they are important. You will gain an understanding of how you can improve your score over time, using case study examples.

Chapter 6 – Your net worth: what it means and why it is important

This short chapter helps you calculate your net worth, and includes some examples to explain why it is an important piece of information to have and use when managing your finances.

Chapter 7 – Reviewing your financial choices I: Bank accounts, interest rates, savings, pensions and property

This chapter takes you through your net worth table, focusing on your investments, savings and the things you own. You will learn about the different bank and building society accounts available to you, how interest rates work, the basics of pensions and investments and how to make financial decisions and choices in this area.

Chapter 8 – Reviewing your financial choices II: Mortgages, credit cards, loans and overdrafts

This chapter explains how debt works and the choices and decisions relating to debt. It covers the basics of mortgages, loans, credit cards and store cards. It also explains the smart way to clear debts, regardless of your credit status.

Chapter 9 – Planning for the life you want I: Financial advice

This chapter answers the question, 'Do I need a financial adviser and how do I choose one?' This chapter will also help you prepare for your first meeting.

Chapter 10 – Planning for the life you want II: Action plan

Assuming that you have worked through the previous chapters and have established your goals and the state of your finances, this chapter gives you a structured way to put together your first action plan. It will help you identify how you can free up wasted money, either to cover your monthly bills, clear up debt or create funds to invest or save for a future event.

Chapter 11 – Making brilliant personal finances a lifelong habit

At this point in the book you will have all the information to start putting together a process that can be used for the rest of your life, regardless of the goal. This chapter introduces the five principles that will give you control over your finances. There are handy templates to help you make straightforward financial decisions, and tips on how to plan and put together a monthly budget and keep track of where you are, using tools already available in your life.

Chapter 12 – Pulling it all together with top tips

This chapter brings together all the learning and tips from the rest of the book. This is a reminder of the steps covered, which can be used as a reference as you use the money management principles to reach your goals. The chapter also includes a section on what you need to do as you reach your reward or goal.

Brilliant resources

At the back of the book you will find a copy of all the tables you may wish to use on an ongoing basis – these are available for you to pull out or copy. There is also a handy reference for all those technical or financial terms that you come across when dealing with financial institutions.

And finally . . .

Not only is the book a good read, it is meant to be your own private workshop. To become brilliant at personal finances, you need to participate. So wherever you are when reading this book make sure you have a pen or pencil in your hand. Be honest with yourself, and remember – to change your life and get what you want, you must take action. Heard that one before? Well, it's true; you actually have to *do* something.

> to get what you want, you must take action

If you are not prepared to participate, then lend this book to someone who is, and get them to give it back to you when they are done; otherwise put the book away until you are ready. Whatever you do, don't take the book back to the shop. You picked it up for a reason! Some nagging reason that you must own up to!

🡕 brilliant action

Table 1.1 is where you can make your own personal action list. This is your own private to-do list for anything you think you need to take action on while reading this book and working through the tasks.

This book is written for people who wish for something more – who want to live differently, stop worrying about money, or just feel more in control.

Now let's get on with it!

Table 1.1 Action list

Topic	Actions needed by me/us

CHAPTER 2

Finding the motivation and reward

Nothing great was ever achieved without enthusiasm.
Ralph Waldo Emerson, American poet and essayist

So you want to be brilliant at managing your personal finances? The big question is *why?*

Becoming brilliant at personal finances takes commitment and action, and needs a reward for your effort. Using the book and developing a lifelong habit requires a positive reason and an understanding of your money personality.

Finding your reason, understanding yourself

Remember I said that you need a pencil with you while reading this book? Now is the time to go and find one if you didn't take me seriously the first time. Before embarking on the first exercise of your personal finances workshop, take a moment to think about why you bought this book. The purpose of the exercise is to find something that will reward you enough to keep you doing something you have not been doing up to now: managing your finances really well.

brilliant tip

To get what you want, you need to know what it is and then focus on getting it. You need to repeat the process of discovering what you want from life at least once a year – and more frequently if your goals are very short term. By using the templates in this chapter you can do this while on the train to work, having a cup of tea in the morning, after a session at the gym, soaking in the bath or while you are in the bathroom for some other reason! In fact you can do this exercise anywhere where you just have a few quiet minutes to yourself while you are waiting for something or someone.

Think about anything you or someone you know has achieved. It may be as simple as getting to the airport on time for your last holiday. Something motivated you to complete the task on time. Getting to the airport on time meant that you did not miss your holiday. You may not have thought about it a great deal but you will have had a specific consequence that motivated you. Our first step, then, is to find your motivation – the consequence of changing your personal finance habits. The first exercise in this book is designed to help you focus your thoughts and help you remove the not so important or urgent reasons from view.

Motivation exercise

Use the blank tables in this chapter to record your thoughts and answers to the following questions. There is a blank version of this exercise at the back of the book that can be copied so that you can complete this with a friend or partner if you are making this a joint effort.

Question 1

What worries me about money and my life?

1   Right now.

2   In the future.

To help you get started, let's use our three case studies as examples. I have chosen one comment from each box. You can write as many as you can think of. It may take a few ideas before you get to the main answer. You may even need to do this more than once before you are happy you have got to the root issue.

 **examples**

Peter:

1   How much of my monthly wages goes towards paying off debts and what will happen if the interest rate rises and the payments go up?

2   How we will be able to pay for all the things we need to keep a family.

Suzanne:

1   Not being in control of my money.

2   Whether I will be too old to travel by the time I earn enough to pay for the ticket. Or, worse, never managing to travel at all.

Rob and Andrew:

1   Making the wrong financial decisions if we ever understand enough to make a decision.

2   Being too cautious about money will mean we will have a boring life.

Table 2.1 Motivation exercise: question 1

What worries me about money and my life?

Now

In the future

Question 2

What does my current money situation stop me doing/having?

1   Right now.

2   In the future.

Again, our case studies are here to help you on your way.

brilliant examples

Peter:

1 Saving for a family.
2 A family.

Suzanne:

1 Setting a date to travel.
2 Travelling.

Rob and Andrew:

1 Starting an independent life.
2 Making future financial decisions.

Table 2.2 Motivation exercise: question 2

What does my current money situation stop me doing/having?

Now

In the future

Question 3

What happens if nothing changes? When I think about money and the future, what do I see?

1 In one year.

2 In five years.

And again, here are the answers from our three case studies.

 **examples**

Peter:

1 More of the same, possibly higher monthly repayments.

2 More debt to pay for the family.

Suzanne:

1 Another birthday where I talk about where I will travel to.

2 Borrowing to travel.

Rob and Andrew:

1 In our own flat but with not much money to spend. Or maybe we will have money to spend? We just don't know how to tell.

2 Can't think that far!

Table 2.3 Motivation exercise: question 3

When I think about money and the future, what do I see?

In one year

In five years

Question 4

When I think about money and the future, what do I want to see?

1   In one year.

2   In five years.

And here are the final answers from our case studies to help you.

 **examples**

Peter:

1   Not so much debt and thinking about starting a family.

2   A family and a bigger house.

Suzanne:

1   Setting a date to travel.

2   Travelling.

Rob and Andrew:

1   A place of our own and an active social life without worrying about money.

2   Being able to plan for later in life and making good financial decisions.

Table 2.4 Motivation exercise: question 4

When I think about money and the future, what do I want to see?

In one year

In five years

Bringing it all together

Well done! I will assume that you have been as honest as you can be with your answers. As with our case study examples, you should find at least one common theme running through

your short-term and long-term comments. Your worries and your wishes surrounding having or lacking money are all to do with

money is a tool to be used to live your life

life. Money is a tool to be used to live your life. If you know how you do and don't want to live your life then you can work out what will reward and motivate you to put together – and stick to – an action plan.

The final part of this exercise is to bring your answers together. Choose one comment from each of the sections: try to collect the most important and those that link together.

If we use Peter as an example, the first thing you notice is that all his answers relate to the amount of debt he has. If you look more closely, the key is the fact that he feels it may stop him from starting a family. Therefore his reward would be planning for a family without the worry of more debt.

My now comments

Question 1

_____

_____

Question 2

_____

_____

Question 3

_____

_____

Question 4

_____

_____

Looking at the above, what is the common theme in *my* answers?

_____

_____

What is *my* short-term reward for being brilliant at personal finances?

_____

_____

My medium-term future comments

Question 1

_____

_____

Question 2

_____

_____

Question 3

_____

_____

Question 4

_____

_____

In the medium-term comments, what is the common theme in _my_ answers?

_____

_____

What is _my_ medium-term reward for being brilliant at personal finances?

_____

_____

My long-term future comments

Finally, make a note of your thoughts on the really long-term view of your life.

Here are some questions to prompt your thoughts:

- When do you want to stop working?
- What sort of education do you need to buy for your children?
- How comfortable do you want to be when you retire?
- Will you need to look after older relatives?
- Do you want to travel or do something spectacular?

_____

_____

_____

_____

_____

You need to have your long-term goals in mind as you make your financial decisions. What works for right now must also work in the long term.

🔼 brilliant action

Now that you have worked out your short- and long-term rewards, write them down and put them where you can read them every day. You need to remind yourself why you are putting the effort in!

- Write them on a reasonable size piece of paper and put them preferably somewhere where you will see them the minute you wake up. One of my workshop attendees put them on the ceiling, as most people wouldn't see them there but she would see them every morning.

- If you use a computer regularly, have your reward written on your screensaver. Another workshop attendee told me he would put 'Life without debt' on his screensaver, as that was his aim.

- If the screensaver idea is too in-your-face or public, get your electronic calendar to send you a reminder every day.

- Use your partner, husband, wife, friends etc. to remind you every now and then of your reward, so that you don't make the wrong decisions. A short text is sometimes all it takes.

- If you use a calendar (desktop or wall) write your reward on every page so that each time you turn to the next month you see it again for the first time.

↗ brilliant recap

- Being brilliant at personal finances requires action and commitment.

- Understanding personal finances and the most financially beneficial decision on its own does not make you brilliant at personal finances.

- You need a reason, reward or at least negative motivation to make you take action.

- Use simple questions with *honest* answers to find the reward that matters.

- Generally there is one reason that is more important than the rest that will give you a reward for changing your habits and taking control.

- You should review your view of life, and how money affects it, at least once a year.

- You can review and plan anywhere that you have a few quiet minutes to yourself.

- Find a way to remind yourself of your goals every day.

CHAPTER 3

Your money personality and why it is important

Everyone ought to bear patiently the results of his own conduct.

Phaedrus, Roman writer of fables

When someone mentions managing money or looking at investments, do you run for the hills or do you feel excited at the prospect of learning something new and prospering from a decision?

Your money personality

How you feel about money is something that should be considered when taking financial decisions. We are not impartial machines or computers. Very few of us take decisions based on the facts alone. Our emotions, past experience, the media and other people's comments all affect our choices.

> our emotions, past experience, the media and other people's comments all affect our choices

Take a simple task such as turning up to meet people. Our personality will affect our ability to get there on time. Some people are naturally organised. They will have checked the timetable of the relevant transport and worked out how long the journey will take, including extra time for delays. They will know exactly what time to leave. But for the rest of us it is sometimes luck that we turn up on the right day, never mind on time. If you know that you always find a last-minute job that has to be done before you leave, or that you are naturally over optimistic on how long everything takes, you can factor this into your decision on when to set off on the journey. In the same way, if you understand how your money personality may affect the development of good personal finance habits, you can avoid making your personal finances journey more difficult than it needs to be.

brilliant example

A person who is highly organised can make the most of a high-interest savings account by moving all surplus money out of their low-interest current bank account on a regular basis and then moving money back when bills are due for payment. But if your personality means that you would forget to move the money back and therefore go overdrawn – or worse still, have your bill payment refused – then this would not be the right personal finance habit for you.

Personality traits you may recognise

Are you a big spender?

Whenever you go to the shops, are you the person who cannot resist buying something you don't actually need or had not planned on? If the answer is yes, you often fit into this category, then you may need to develop some simple habits to ensure that your money is getting you where you want to go rather than where you wander.

This personality trait may not cause you hardship if your income is high enough to support your actions; in which case you may not even notice the habit and how much money is potentially wasted. But you may be like our case study Suzanne. You may have a dream to travel but your spending habits stop you from realising your dream. If the reason is big enough, then you can develop habits to counteract your spending behaviour. Think about the last time you went shopping and bought something non-essential. Did you really need it and was there something else that you could, and probably should, have done with the money?

brilliant tip

What you don't have, you don't miss! If your spending willpower is very low and you want to save, then put in place something that takes the money before you see it. Take part in a save-as-you-earn scheme or set up a standing order effective on pay day to transfer money to a savings account. When you plan not to spend money, leave all your plastic spending power at home. Only take enough cash to pay for the things you need.

Do you find it hard to part with money?

Do you find yourself giving these excuses?

- About the pair of shoes you have had for 10 years: '*They haven't worn out yet – why would I get new ones?*'

- About the dining room table that is almost falling apart: '*We could fix that, there is no need to spend on a new one.*'

- About the visit abroad to see family and friends: '*Won't that be really expensive – can't we just call instead?*'

Being careful with your money is not a bad thing, especially if there is not enough to go around. However, always focusing on the cost of living your life can mean that you don't actually live the life you want. If this personal finance habit is one you recognise, using the results of Chapter 2 – your goals and rewards – will help you to balance your spending decisions.

brilliant example

Andrew's parents, Sheila and Bill, live mortgage and debt free. Bill had a successful software design company and sold his shares when he retired. He is very careful and has a very healthy pension provision – more than they can spend – but he is afraid of being broke. Sheila had a good corporate job and has a company pension she took when she retired early. They both agreed that when they retired their goal was to take time out and really enjoy their favourite pastimes. Sheila loves to read, Bill loves to watch sport. Sheila is always saying that she would like to have a conservatory so that she can sit and read in a pleasant environment rather than in the room where Bill watches sport. Bill, although he agrees they can easily afford it, says if they keep dipping into their savings for things they don't really need then one day there will be nothing left.

Sheila and Bill both had a life goal. When considering the decision to spend their savings on a conservatory, Bill has not considered Sheila's goal. Assuming that the cost of the conservatory will not detrimentally affect their retirement, it would appear that it is Bill's fear of not having enough money that affects his financial decision making.

brilliant tip

When you hear yourself arguing against a sensible purchase, ask yourself 'How will this decision help me achieve my/our short-, medium- and long-term goal?' You need to live for today *and* tomorrow, not just one or the other.

Are you always the one that pays?

Is this you?

- You organise a group outing and do not ask for the money from members of the group. (You are too embarrassed to ask if people don't offer.)
- You feel people will think less of you if you are not generous when out.
- You never feel you have spent enough on presents.
- People always come to your place for dinner or entertainment.

Being generous is not a bad thing unless it is excessive and affects your goals in life. If you recognise yourself from the comments, ask yourself if this is justified. Look again at your goals and see if this side of your money personality is affecting your ability to reach your reward. There are small changes that you can make so that you are protected from feeling embarrassed and still pay your fair share. For example, getting payment upfront for a group outing saves embarrassment and makes sure no one is disadvantaged.

brilliant example

Suzanne wanted to save up for a car. She didn't want to stay in all the time and miss going out with her friends but she found that her social spending left her with too little each month to save. She realised that she would offer to organise tickets to local concerts and often would buy more rounds of drinks or snacks than anyone else. It wasn't that her friends didn't want to pay their share; it was more that she would insist or get there first. She decided that she would focus just on the tickets. Also, when she organised the next concert trip she explained that she had been saving for her car and so did not have the money to get the tickets upfront. All her friends were more than happy to give her the money to buy the tickets so that she ▶

could still do a great job of organising the evening. She found that by changing her approach to spending and organising her social life meant that she could save on average an extra £80 a month without changing her lifestyle. Not enough to buy the car, but it was a start.

Suzanne found that by recognising that she felt embarrassed asking for money after the event, she could change the way she organised nights out so that she was protected from her own habits. If you fit into this category, think about the last time you felt you overspent. Could you have organised things differently?

How safe do you need to feel?

Which one are you?

- **No risk please**: If you have savings plans or pensions that are linked to the stock market, you worry about them all the time. When making a financial decision, you need to make sure that everything is guaranteed, even though this may cost you more money or take longer to get the income or return you want.

- **Any risk for the reward**: You just want the biggest money return from your investment and don't worry if you lose the lot. The risk is worth the gamble.

- **Somewhere in between**: You are prepared to take some risk but also like to know that some of your money is safe.

This is your attitude to risk. It is extremely important that you are honest about how comfortable you are with financial decisions. Some people fall into the first category simply because they do not understand what will happen to their money. If this is you, then take particular note of the information in the chapters dealing with planning for your life and dealing with financial advisers.

brilliant tip

When faced with a financial decision, take expert advice. Make sure that the adviser or salesperson explains in plain English the worst-case outcome. If you are comfortable with the worst-case outcome, then you will not feel the need to worry about your decision. If worrying about the risk affects your life too much, then don't do it. Look for another way.

You may find that some of these habits or personality traits apply and some do not. The next exercise will help you to focus on the ones that sometimes apply to you and the possible consequences on your financial life. Look at each 'money personality' in Table 3.1 and tick the ones that apply. Use the 'impact on your life' comments as an extra guide if you are not sure.

Table 3.1 What is your money personality?

Your money personality	Tick	Impact on your life
I can't resist buying something when I am out		You probably have quite a few store cards and credit cards, with balances on all of them
I never feel I have enough money put aside, even though I know I have		This probably affects other members of your family more than you; you may feel guilty about not living
I would not like to risk losing my investment		You probably do not have investments in the stock market; if you do, you worry about them
I would always take the gamble for the highest return		The impact will depend on how lucky you are
I like to gamble a bit, but also keep some safe		This is a balanced view, and with the right information and decision-making tools it can lead to a stress-free life
I feel people will think I am mean if I don't pay more than my share or buy big enough presents		You never any spare money to save and you may borrow to keep up appearances; you probably have an overdraft, and use credit cards to pay for social events and presents

brilliant tips

- If you want to save for the future but can't resist retail therapy, then save before you get your money. Use a company saving scheme or set up a standing order for savings to come out of your bank account on pay day.

- Not spending money when you can afford to is reducing the pleasure of living. Find someone with the opposite personality to help you talk through the positive reasons for your spending decision. Ask yourself: 'Will I still be able to afford to meet my financial commitments and will this decision contribute towards achieving my goals?'

- If you are always over-generous, remember that it can affect your own future. Sometimes try not to be the first to offer to pay. When organising a group trip, get everyone to pay upfront for tickets. When out with a group for the night, suggest a kitty.

- Understand your attitude to financial risk. When planning investments, if you verge on the safe side then remember that you may not be able to go for the biggest return in the shortest time. You may need longer planning time to reach your goal. If you verge more towards the risky side, have a contingency in your plan in case it all goes wrong. Make sure you can manage if you take a gamble and then lose your investment.

brilliant recap

- Many of your current financial decisions and money management habits are dictated by your money personality.

- This personality may be based on early life experiences or just your make-up.

- For a balanced view and approach to money management and financial decision making, you need to understand and at times contradict your money personality.

- In order to achieve your goal, you may have to ignore the urge to spend on items that are not a necessity, or go against your frugal nature and spend savings on something that will meet a life goal for you, your partner or your family.

And finally ...

Now you have started to think about your money personality, ask someone you trust to confirm your view and add anything you may not have thought about that influences the way you deal with money and financial decisions.

CHAPTER 4

Discovering the state of your finances

Why is there so much month left at the end of the money?

Anonymous

B y the end of this chapter you will understand how to check your personal finances on a regular basis. We are now on the second step of your personal finances journey.

Figure 4.1 Continuing on your journey

In any journey you need to know at least two things:

1 Where you want to get to.
2 Where you are now.

Then you can find the quickest and easiest route between the two.

In Chapter 2 you worked out where you want to be in the short and medium term. This chapter helps you work out where you are now.

First, remind yourself why you are doing this. Write down the short- and medium-term reason or reward that you discovered in Chapter 2 (see pages 25–26).

_____

_____

_____

_____

Do you know where the money goes?

If we were really in a workshop situation, I would now be asking you to tell me if you know where your money goes each month.

Well, do you? The obvious answers are:

- Yes.
- No.
- Er . . . I think so.
- My husband/wife/partner/sister/brother/mum . . . or someone other than me takes care of that.
- Why do I need to?

If you plan just to bumble your way through life and see if you are lucky enough to survive, then you would probably not have picked up this book in the first place. So have a pencil at the ready and your mind in gear.

You are now going to complete a 10-minute financial health check. You will do this by completing the tables in the next few pages from memory or perception. If you can't remember, give it your best guess.

And why should you do this? To see how in control of your finances you really are and to help you see how much work there is to do to reach your goal.

Where does the money come from?

Table 4.1 is about your income. The table has three columns. These represent the previous three months of your life. In each column, fill in the amount you actually received for each category. When you have finished, go down column one and add all the figures for Month 1 together, and put the total at the bottom of the column in the 'Total' row. Do the same for Month 2 and Month 3.

Table 4.1 Income

My income	Month 1	Month 2	Month 3
Salary 1			
Salary 2			
Freelance income 1			
Freelance income 2			
State benefits			
Pension			
Maintenance			
Child support			
Investment income			
Rental income			
Other			
Other			
TOTAL			

Where does the money go?

Your fixed expenses

First, you need to look at the money going out that is absolutely fixed. There are two reasons it is fixed: you have no choice about paying it, or you have chosen to spend it and are under contract. This does not mean that you can't reduce the payments by getting a better deal, but right now this is what you must pay. In Table 4.2 expenses have been grouped together under a common heading. Write down your estimate of how much you have spent in each category over the last three months.

Before completing Table 4.2 take a look at what to include in each category:

- **Utilities**: Water bills, gas bills, electricity bills, cesspit bills, oil, any other fuels.
- **Rent and service**: Monthly rent, service charges.
- **Mortgage**: The monthly payment, any extra fees.
- **Insurances**: Car insurance, house insurance, life insurance, health insurance, sickness and accident insurance (not travel insurance).
- **Communication**: Landline phone, mobile phones (if on contract), internet.
- **Food**: Basic foods (not eating out).
- **Transport**: Trains, buses, car tax, petrol, car maintenance.
- **Medical**: Regular medical bills, medicines.
- **Child-related**: School fees, school food, child-minding fees, school trips, clothes.
- **Debt payments**: Loan repayments.
- **Finance charges**: Credit card late payment charges and interest charges, late payment fines, parking fines, travel fines, any other not-keeping-to-the-rules fines.

- **Investments and savings**: Pensions, savings plans (these can be considered discretionary: include them here if you have set up a standing order or some formal payment plan).
- **One-off items**: For any once-a-year payment, assume that you have to save towards it: take the amount, divide by 12 and put that amount in each month, just as if you were spending it.

As with Table 4.1, when completed add all the items in the Month 1 column together and put the total in the last 'Total' row, and do the same again for Month 2 and Month 3.

Table 4.2 Fixed spending

No choice: money out	Month 1	Month 2	Month 3
Utilities			
Rent and service			
Mortgage			
Insurances			
Communication			
Food			
Transport			
Medical			
Child-related			
Debt payments			
Finance charges			
Investments and savings			
One-off items			
TOTAL			

Discretionary expenses – spending you have a choice about

In your quest to find out where the money goes, Table 4.3 focuses on items over which you have some choice. This is normally the bit of spending that makes your stressful life less like hard work and more like fun. It is also the area that, when things get tough, most people borrow to afford.

Before completing Table 4.3 take a look at what to include in each category:

- **Eating and drinking**: All eating and drinking out, including coffees, sandwiches, burgers, etc.
- **Gambling and tobacco**: All cigarettes, cigars, loose tobacco, lottery, scratch cards, raffle tickets.
- **Household**: All cleaning products and general maintenance, cleaner, ironing, window cleaners, gardening costs, household bills not included anywhere else.
- **Subscriptions**: Magazines, satellite or cable TV, DVDs, books, gym fees.
- **Activities**: Theme parks, leisure activities, films, shows, clubs.
- **Reading**: Book and magazine purchases (not part of a subscription).
- **Music**: CDs, downloads, music subscriptions.
- **Travel**: Holidays, special trips.
- **Pets**: Food, insurance, toys, luxuries, vet bills.
- **Grooming**: Hairdresser, nail bar, facials, tanning, waxing, barber, any other beauty treatments.
- **Occasions**: Birthdays, special holidays where gifts are given, weddings, religious occasions, family occasions, any other occasion.
- **Clothes and accessories**: Include all those small bargains.
- **Investments and savings**: Pensions, savings plans (these can be considered discretionary: include them here if you

feel that you are prepared to change the amount you pay into your pension or saving plan based on your life goals).

● **One-off items**: For any once-a-year payment, assume that you have to save towards it: take the amount, divide by 12 and put that amount in each month, just as if you were spending it.

Table 4.3 Discretionary spending

Your choice: money out	Month 1	Month 2	Month 3
Eating and drinking			
Gambling and tobacco			
Household			
Subscriptions			
Activities			
Reading			
Music			
Travel			
Pets			
Grooming			
Occasions			
Clothes and accessories			
Investments and savings			
One-off items			
Other			
TOTAL			

Making sense of the numbers

Brilliant work. Now that you know how to fill in the numbers from memory, it doesn't take long to put the actual number in.

But, I hear you say, 'So what?'. Well, here is what . . . You now need to put the totals somewhere where you can see if your spending habits over the last three months are getting you where you want to go.

So, pencils at the ready . . . let's fill in the last bit. Take the totals of each column of Tables 4.1, 4.2 and 4.3 and copy them in Table 4.4. The first column of Table 4.4 tells you what to do.

Table 4.4 Spending habits

How to work it out	Summary	Month 1	Month 2	Month 3
A: Copy from Table 4.1 total	Total: money in			
B: Copy from Table 4.2 total	Total: fixed spending			
C: Take row B amount away from row A amount	Money left for discretionary spending			
D: Copy from Table 4.3 total	Total: discretionary spending			
E: Take row D amount away from row C amount	Money left over or overspent			

What does it all mean?

Let's reflect on where you think you are. Does Table 4.4 show that you have money left over or does it show that you have spent more than you earn?

Now you have the information written down, and you know what you want, you can decide what to do. What do the results show about you?

1   You have money left over each month. If this feels right, then what are you doing with it to meet your goals?

2   You have money left over. If it does not feel that way, then you need to track your real spending. Then fill in these tables based on fact rather than memory to see what spending you have left out.

3   You have money left over but not enough to get the reward you are looking for.

4   You are spending more than you earn. This means you are heading for more debt and probably not getting your reward.

In the case of 3 and 4 you need to find ways of either increasing your income or reducing your spending. You will find help on how to do this in Chapters 10 and 11. Go back to Table 4.2 and Table 4.3 and see where you think you may spend more than you want. Draw a nice circle around the numbers you want to reduce so that you can come back to them later in the book.

↗ brilliant recap

In this chapter you have:

● discovered that you have time to analyse your spending;

● focused the mind on where you think your money comes from and where it goes;

● split your spending into two parts:
  – things you have no choice about;
  – things you choose to spend on;

● discovered whether you spend more than you earn or just more than you can afford;

● understood that you need to take action to get your reward;

● highlighted areas that you think you could spend less on.

Knowing what you actually do with your money gives you the power to make decisions that can change your life.

CHAPTER 5

Understanding your credit score and how to influence it

Knowledge is power if you know it about the right person.
Ethel Watts Mumford, American writer

What an organisation knows about you shapes their decision. The question is, what do they know?

We have come some way on our journey towards being brilliant with personal finances. Before we move on, let's recap on where we have been.

- You have worked out where you are financially.
- You have decided where you would like to be and how you would like to feel about your finances.
- You have looked at your money personality and how that affects your financial situation.

Now we are going to take a look at you through the eyes of a potential lender.

When you want to borrow money or buy anything on credit, you are assessed and given a *credit score*. In this chapter you will learn about credit scores, how to check your credit report and how to take action to ensure you have the best score possible.

brilliant definition

Credit score

The number given to you by a credit agency or potential lender, based on information provided by you, other lenders and public offices such as the local authority council and courts of law. This score is used to rate how risky you are in terms of personal finance management.

The main reason for understanding your credit score is so that you can understand how financial institutions view the risk they take when dealing with you as a customer or potential debtor.

Financial institutions or organisations that deal with the general public are banks, building societies and companies that provide finance for all the goods and services you want to buy, but pay for later. If the organisation that you want to deal with believes that there is a chance they may not get their money back on time – or at all – they will want a bigger reward for the risk they are taking. After all, would you lend money to a stranger without enough reward to make it worth your while? Follow that train of thought and you will agree that a person considered high risk would not be offered the cheapest deals. On the other hand, being considered a low financial risk gets you the best deals and stretches your money further!

being considered a low financial risk gets you the best deals

Your credit score and keeping your side of the bargain

Imagine you were to become a money lender. Let's consider the three commonsense results that would be important to you:

1 The person you lend money to pays you back in full, as agreed.

2 You receive an acceptable reward in return for your trouble.

3 If the person does not pay you back, you have another way of getting your money.

What information and documents would you need in place to achieve these results?

Result 1: The person you lend money to pays you back in full, as agreed

A legally binding agreement (*contract*) between the lender and the debtor – 'the small print' – is often seen as the way to make sure that both sides have agreed when and how the money should be paid.

Contracts and legal agreements don't always come in documents marked 'contract'. Whenever we fill in an application to open an account you often see the words: 'by signing this application you agree to abide by the terms and conditions set out on page . . .'. Usually you find this very close to the signature box. You sign in the box and send off the application and this means that you have entered into a contract that will be binding unless you cancel the agreement within the time legally allowed.

How often have you signed something, including a credit card application, without actually reading the small print? When asked, most people admit that they do not read the terms and conditions when applying for a mobile phone, a credit card or the interest-free finance deal on offer with their purchase. Of the many reasons given, the three most popular answers are:

- If I read it, I would not understand it anyway.
- I didn't have my glasses with me and the writing was too small.
- I just did not have time to sit and read every word.

If you don't read the terms and conditions, that is your choice. I don't want to scare you, but when you sign these agreements you *are* agreeing to your side of the bargain. Generally you are also stating that you have read and understood the terms and conditions you have not yet read.

Imagine this conversation between Rob and a mobile phone supplier.

Rob	I want to have one of your wiggle woggle mobile phones on monthly contract.
Mobile phone supplier	Of course, sir. You need to sign this application form. Let me explain what you must do to keep to your part of the contract and the penalties that will come your way if you do not.
Rob	No thanks. If by chance my normal habits mean I break the agreement, you can charge me whatever the penalty happens to be. I like surprises.

It sounds quite ridiculous, doesn't it? But this is exactly the response you are giving when you don't read the terms and conditions.

So, to emphasise the point: the terms and conditions tell you what you are agreeing to and what will happen if you do not keep to the agreement. They will also tell you how long you have to cancel your application without any penalty. The simple habit of asking 'Can you please explain the small print?' every time you are asked to sign something will mean you are well informed and saves you reading stuff you don't understand.

brilliant example

Rob received a letter through the post from his bank offering him a credit card. The letter and application form said that it was a 'personal invitation to a world of treats'. It offered a number of rewards and points towards days out and travel-related purchases. The double-sided application form provided space and boxes for Rob to fill in his personal details on one side, with a full page of small print with headings such as 'Key financial information', 'Your right to cancel', 'Key information' and 'Your personal information' on the other. The page did not say 'legally binding contract' at the top, but did state just above the signature box: 'This is a credit agreement regulated by the Consumer Credit Act 1974. Sign it only if you want to be legally bound by its terms'.

Rob thought he would read the small print information later, which of course he did not. Rob's signature confirmed that he had read the terms and conditions and *agreed* to them. Rob's application was accepted and he received his credit card within two weeks. Rob did not keep track of his spending and went over his credit limit in the first month. He also forgot to make the first payment on time. Rob's first statement showed two additional charges of £12 each. Rob called the credit card company and asked what the charges were for. The credit card company confirmed that he had agreed to the terms and conditions. They stated that they would charge a £12.00 account supervision fee when he missed the minimum payment or went above his credit limit.

What Rob did not consider was that his application was a legally binding contract and he had not kept his side of the bargain. Not reading the terms and conditions meant that Rob was now £24 more out of pocket than he had planned to be, with nothing to show for it.

You may not think that £24 is a great deal of money and that Rob will have learned his lesson the hard way. However, being in control of your personal finances is about getting what you want from your money. It was not Rob's intention to throw away £24. Rob's ignorance of the terms and his bad financial habit had the same effect as him going out into the street and giving away £24 to a stranger for no reason. Rob had a goal – his own home and independence; surely the £24 could have been put to better use elsewhere and helped him to achieve his goal. Lazy financial habits make the road to achieving your life and financial goals much longer.

> lazy financial habits make the road to achieving your goals much longer

Credit agreements exercise

Remember that pen or pencil you had at the beginning of the book. Grab it now and get ready for another exercise. As with the previous exercises, try to complete this from memory and then follow up by checking the actual documents for the real answers. The point of this task is to make you aware of the agreements you have entered into and give you a handy one-page list that you can use to help set up automatic payments. This will make sure you never throw away money by just not being organised enough to pay your bills on time.

In the first column of Table 5.1, write down the name of all the credit cards, store cards, bank loans or finance agreements you have. In the second column write the penalty that you would be charged if you are late or miss a payment. In the third column write the date you are due to make your next monthly payment.

Table 5.1 Credit agreements

Credit card, store card, loan or finance agreement	Late payment penalty	Date next payment is due

brilliant tip

If you are regularly being charged for late payments or for going above your agreed credit or overdraft limit, look at your statements for the last six months, add up all your charges and find something you could have bought or done with the money. This will give you a good reason for being more organised. In Rob's case, a late payment charge of £12 each month adds up to £144 a year. Enough to pay for a late deal autumn break for one in the Canaries or for the annual car tax on a small car. Avoid late charges by setting up a direct debit for the minimum payment each month. You can always make an extra payment if you can afford to pay more than the minimum required.

brilliant definition

Direct debit

An instruction or order given by the bank or building society's account holder to the bank or building society to pay a particular organisation the amount they demand on an agreed regular basis.

Now we have established that the legally binding terms and conditions are one way that lenders use to get you to agree when and how to pay the money back, let's move on to the next result a money lender might look for.

Result 2: You receive an acceptable reward in return for your trouble

How do you work out what is an acceptable reward? Easy! Start with the minimum you want based on the perfect result, then crank it up the less likely you are to get a perfect result.

It is often said that past performance is an indication of the future. Looking at whether or not someone has kept to their word in the past is a good indication of the risk you are taking. This is exactly the process financial institutions follow. They require independent proof that you are good at managing money and keeping to agreements.

Q Where do organisations get their information about you and your financial performance?

A Three credit reference agencies.

brilliant definition

Credit reference agency

An organisation that has a legal right to keep a record of the credit history, payment performance and related identity information of individuals. It makes this information available to anyone planning to offer credit to the individual, *provided they have permission and the right to see the information*.

The three credit agencies used in the UK are:

- **Equifax**, PO Box 1140, Bradford, BD1 5US (www.equifax.co.uk)

- **Experian**, PO Box 9000, Nottingham, NG80 7WP (www.experian.co.uk)

- **Callcredit**, PO Box 491, Leeds, LS3 1WZ (www.callcredit.co.uk)

Just a few instances where you will complete some form of application and provide personal details to an organisation are when you:

- want to make a large purchase with credit or some form of delayed payment;

- apply to open a bank account;

- want to buy a property and apply to take out a mortgage;

- apply for a credit card;

- want to rent a property;

- apply for a mobile phone contract.

A few pages ago we mentioned the small print, the terms and conditions, in an agreement. In these terms and conditions is a section about your personal information. By submitting your application, you have given permission for the organisation to search the records kept by one or all of the credit reference agencies.

Where do credit agencies get their information?

Credit agencies have arrangements with all financial institutions to receive information about the credit agreements they enter into with members of the public. Among some of the information they keep are:

- a record of statement balances and the value and timings of payments made to them;
- information from the electoral register;
- the Register of Judgments;
- orders and fines;
- information provided by you and anyone you are financially associated with.

All this information is updated at least once a month.

Credit agencies do not compile a list of people who should not be given credit. Credit agencies only supply factual information; the decision about whether or not credit should be given is left to the organisation that is processing the application.

 brilliant definitions

Electoral register

A list of all people who have registered and are eligible to vote in UK political elections. The register confirms their current address and that the voter is over 18.

Register of Judgments, Orders and Fines

Registry Trust Limited holds and provides information about court judgments held against a person for non-payment of a debt. This information is made available to the credit agencies for inclusion in their credit reports.

Financial associate

Someone with whom you have a financial link, such as a joint bank account or mortgage. Their details will be included in your credit report so that a lender can check their payment performance and use this as part of their analysis of your risk as a debtor.

Organisations use this information to decide how reliable you are. If they think you are too unreliable then they will refuse to enter into a financial relationship with you at all, and your application will be refused.

Influencing your credit score

You are a credit score number. It is this that determines the answer to the question: 'Can I have credit and how much will it cost?' Every organisation will have a different method of coming up with your credit score – and they do not have to tell you how they calculate it. Generally the score will be on a rising scale running from 0 to 1,000. The lowest number indicates a poor credit score and the highest number indicates an excellent credit score. A low credit score generally means that you are high risk and unreliable.

Let's follow the logic then. High risk means you will be more trouble, and more trouble means more reward needed. Alternatively, to obtain credit at the lowest cost, you must appear to be as stable and reliable as possible. And so the answer stares us in the face: make yourself look low risk!

> to obtain credit at the lowest cost, you must appear to be reliable

The aim is to get to the highest score. To get the highest score your credit report needs to say:

- I am stable, reliable and honest.
- I don't associate with financially bad people.
- I don't have too much credit.
- I am not trying to borrow as much money as possible and run off with it.
- I am so organised that if you make a mistake I will get you to fix it pronto.

How can you make your report say all of the above?

I am stable, reliable and honest, but how can I prove it?

Step 1: Prove who you are and where you live

As part of your application you may have to show some form of identification, so having a passport or driving licence or a bill that is addressed specifically to you will give some confidence. The other piece of information that makes the organisation feel warm and comfortable about your stability sits on your *credit report*.

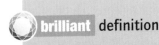 **brilliant** definition

Credit report

A report prepared by credit reference agencies, with a summary of all the information they have been provided with or gather about you and your financial performance.

The report will detail where you live now and where you have lived in the past and when you were registered to vote. So if you have not registered to vote, you are likely to lose points. Organisations believe you live at an address if the council confirms it. This provides the independent proof they need. Living in the same place for at least three years also gives you extra points.

Let's assess your stability. Using Table 5.2, fill in the addresses you have lived at or have had bills and statements sent to in the last three years. In the second column place a tick if you were registered to vote from the time you moved in. In the third column put a cross if you can't prove you lived there.

Table 5.2 Proof of where you live

Address	Registered to vote from moving in	Can't prove I lived there

How did you do? Which of the following results is true for you?

- You have lived in more than three addresses in three years and you have not always let the council know where you are for their voting register. Points lost! Why? Well, if you miss your payments and you have also moved it will cost the organisation more money to find you and get you to settle your debt. They need more reward for that.

- You have lived at more than three addresses in three years but have always updated the electoral register. Not so many points lost this time. You may not be the most stable person in the world, but at least if you move they can find you, talk to you and get their money back!

- You have lived at the same address for three years and updated the electoral register when you moved. Bingo! You will get the most points for stability in terms of residence.

A question: you are not old enough to vote and still live at home, where you have lived for at least 17 years. What will the organisation make of that?

Young people often have limited proof of their address because they still live at home. Unless they have bills of their own or are registered to vote, then there is no independent proof of where they live. However, with the support of their parents, there are ways to organise the household finances so that they can provide proof and begin to provide information for their credit score. Of course, if the parents have a good credit score then they can provide a guarantee for their son or daughter.

brilliant example

Before Andrew went to university he had always lived with his parents. He did not have a passport and did not drive. As he had only just turned 18 he also was not yet registered to vote. With no bills in his name and no documentation to prove where he lived, Andrew was considered high risk. Andrew had a part-time job to contribute towards his keep. Instead of paying for food, his contribution went towards the household bills. Andrew's parents chose the smallest monthly bill and arranged to switch it to Andrew's name; they had to guarantee that if he did not pay then they would pay the bill themselves. Effectively they would make sure the bill was paid on time. Andrew now had proof of address using a household bill. He built up a good payment record that would reduce how risky he appeared on his credit report, which up to now had been blank.

Another problem might be having to move often because of work. Moving home frequently does affect your credit score, but not as much as not being registered to vote at the address you have moved to, and not as much as bad payment history. So it is not the end of the world if you need to move often.

 **tip**

If you are moving away from your home for a period of time but then returning, consider just redirecting mail to the new address rather than making it a permanent move.

Step 2: Keep to your agreements

Here is a big question. Do you consider yourself a reliable person who keeps their promises?

You do not need to write the answer to that one in the book. I am sure you are more than capable of thinking about the question and answering it. If the answer is yes, then let's see whether or not good intentions translate into reality. Look at how well you keep to your agreements. What agreements? Well, the financial ones providing you with credit of course!

Be really honest in the next exercise. You are the only one who is looking at it and you will miss the point if you fib to yourself. You are going to create a list of all the financial agreements you have entered into in the last six years and then comment on how well you have kept to them.

> you will miss the point if you fib to yourself

In Table 5.3, moving from left to right, put a brief description of the credit agreement in the first column: remember to include all the credit cards and store cards you have, even if you no longer use them. In the second column write how long you have had the agreement. Place a tick in the third column if you have ever been late with a payment or in some way not kept to the

Table 5.3 Credit record

Credit agreements in last six years that you have not cancelled (loans, credit/store cards, mobile phone contract, rental and finance agreements for goods and services)	How long have you had the agreement?	Have you ever broken the agreement?	Number of times paid late in the past 12 months	Number of times paid three months late in the last six years
Peter's Barclaycard (credit card)	5 years	✓	1	5

That was not so bad, was it? Look at the table again. Have you missed anything?

agreement. In the fourth column write the number of times you have been late, even by one day, making payments in the last 12 months. Finally, if you can remember, put the number of times you have been more than three months late making a payment in the last six years. I know that is a long time, but give it a go.

And why are you completing this exercise? It is so that you get a feel for some of the information potential lenders look at when deciding whether or not to refuse your application. I've filled in the first line using the Barclaycard agreement of our case study Peter, to give you an example to follow.

Now go and complete Table 5.3 based on your own information before continuing to read the rest of this chapter.

The completed table represents just some of the information an organisation will see when they view your credit report. If you have at least a couple of agreements named on the list and all the other columns are empty, then you are on your way to full points on your credit score. For most people this is not the case.

The important thing to know is that bad payment history can stay on your credit report for six years. This is especially true if you had the agreement cancelled and had to be taken to court to recover the debt. Court judgments and bankruptcies stay on your credit report until satisfied and clear. Most credit reports give detailed information about the last 12 months' behaviour. Your account is considered *delinquent*, just like a badly behaved child, if payments are regularly late or there is a payment more than three months late. You will be in default if you stop paying altogether and the agreement has been cancelled.

If, when you look at Table 5.3, you can see that your payment history is not good, then start now and work your way towards being reliable and keeping to your payment dates. The longer you go without missing a payment date, the more points go towards your credit score. If you can't remember to pay on time, then set up a direct debit or standing order to make sure you pay the minimum amount required on the day it is due.

 action

Use Table 5.3 as a tool to improve your credit score. Make a copy of the page and put it somewhere where you will look at it at least once a month. Start with the entries in the 12-month column; as you progress and the time without missing a payment on that particular agreement exceeds 12 months, then cross out your entry. Promise yourself a small reward for each crossed out entry. When you have crossed out all the 12-month column entries, throw the paper away and give yourself a final reward.

I don't associate with financially bad people

A financial associate is someone who you are financially linked to. You may have a joint bank account, a joint mortgage, joint insurance policy or some other joint financial undertaking. This information will be recorded and sent to the credit reference agencies and will then be available to any organisation authorised to search your records.

The fact that you are associated financially means that an organisation will then want to check the credit risk of the person you are associated with. In the same way that parents believe that if their child mixes in bad company then they will be influenced to behave badly, the organisation looking at your application will take points away for the bad behaviour of your financial associates. Your good score does not drag theirs up; their bad score drags yours down.

 **example**

Peter and Helen's first home was a rented flat. Helen had previously lived at home with her parents. When they first moved in, Helen went out to rent a TV for the flat: a cheap £12-a-month TV until they decided what to buy. Helen had a good job and no debts, but to her surprise her application was refused. Apparently her credit score was not high enough. She was too high risk for the rental company. Peter had never asked Helen about her finances or credit score, even though it could have an impact on his life. The TV rental company confirmed which credit reference agency they used. A copy of Helen's credit report showed there was no credit history at all. Helen could prove who she was and where she lived, but had no credit history because she did not have any credit/store cards or even a mobile phone.

The reason Helen's score was so low was because the credit reference agency just did not know if she was the sort of person who would pay on time or not. Helen provided more information to the rental company and they reversed their decision. Peter and Helen wanted to buy a house at some point in the future and now realised that, because both their credit scores would be considered, they needed to get Helen's credit score improved so that jointly they had a chance of obtaining the best mortgage deals.

Interesting story, but what about you? Use Table 5.4 to write down who you are financially associated with and how. Then decide whether or not you think they have a good credit history or not. The hard part will be asking them about their credit history to see if you are right.

Table 5.4 Financial associates

Name of associate connected	How you are credit history	Good or bad

brilliant tip

Before opening a joint account with someone for convenient bill payments, consider their financial behaviour. If it is not as reliable as yours, then split the bill payments equally between you instead. For example, one person will pay the gas bill and the other person will pay the electricity bill, and so on. At the end of each month or quarter check to see that there is a fair 50/50 split. Make sure that the bills you are each actually paying are in your respective names. This way, late payments only affect the credit report of the person whose name is on the bill.

What if you have already created a financial association and now have reason to regret it? There are three options available:

● break your association;
● work on improving the other person's credit history and score;
● carry on as you are and continue to be penalised for not having the best credit score.

However, the third option should really be crossed out, assuming you really want to improve your personal finances. And if you have joint financial commitments such as a mortgage then the first option on the list is probably not the easiest way forward. In this case you need to work with the person you are associated with by using this chapter and the various guidance available from *all* three credit reference agencies to improve their credit score.

I don't have too much credit

Having too much credit available, even if you are not currently using it, will reduce your chances of successfully applying for credit that you actually need.

Think about this from the point of view of the money lender. Imagine you have £10,000 worth of credit card debt available to you today but are only using £2,000 worth. Tomorrow you can get up, go on a shopping spree and spend another £8,000. In one day your debt can go from £2,000 to £10,000. Your monthly repayments will also increase, leaving you with less in your pocket available to pay for anything else.

Organisations looking at your application for finance will again award points based on your level of available credit. They will have their own idea of how much you could comfortably afford, based on the income information you have supplied. They don't know that the loyalty card you took out in 1995, the one that you lost down the back of the sofa and never renewed, with an available credit limit of £1,000, will never be used again. If you did not cancel the account then you could, in theory, go out today and spend £1,000 without anyone questioning your actions.

Time to review. Look back to the information you recorded in Table 5.3 on page 70. Look at the list of credit cards and store cards and answer the following questions.

Did you leave out cards that are no longer in your bag or wallet but have never been cancelled? If the answer is yes, quickly jot down the ones you can remember in the next section.

List the cards no longer used here.

_____

_____

_____

_____

From your list of cards, which of the cards have a zero balance?

_____

_____

_____

_____

How many of those cards do you no longer need?

_____

_____

_____

_____

If you think there are more credit or store cards but you are not sure, then come back to these questions again after we talk about checking your credit report on page 79.

You may be very pleased with yourself because you have written zero or none in the answer to the last two questions. Don't be too smug though. Just because you don't have any zero-balance cards doesn't mean you don't have too much credit. It may mean that you are just using too much of it, but that is the subject of another chapter. If you have zero-balances on cards that you no longer have, or use, you need to take some action. Before you do, however, there is another question you need to answer.

On each of the cards or credit accounts, did you ever miss payments?

- **Yes**: You need to see if those missed payments still appear on your credit report. If they do, you need to wait until those missed payments drop off the report, otherwise they will stay there for six years.

- **No**: You can go ahead and close the account you no longer need.

brilliant tip

If you want to get rid of an old store or credit card you no longer use, and which has a zero outstanding balance but has a bad payment history, don't close the account until the missed payment history drops off your credit report. Also, contact the organisation and ask for your credit limit to be reduced to the lowest value possible. Work out when your bad payment history will disappear and put a note in your calendar or diary, or if you use an electronic reminder add this as a forward date, to remind you to cancel the card or account.

I am not trying to borrow as much money as possible and run off with it

brilliant example

Suzanne decided she needed a credit card to help her get through buying all those presents for Christmas. She was pretty good at navigating her way around the internet and decided to check out the special credit card deals that were available giving 0% interest for three months. She was not sure which one would be the best one to choose, so she sat down one evening with a mug of coffee and applied for six all at once. She felt very pleased ▶

with herself and started to write up the Christmas shopping list. Then the replies started to come back. The first application was accepted but the remaining companies rejected her applications. Some asked for more information and confirmation of her identity and some offered her a different but not so good deal. She didn't understand why she was good enough for one company but not the rest.

What Suzanne did not realise was that each time one of the credit card organisations processed her application they made a search on her credit report. Each subsequent company could see how many searches had been made recently. The fact that she had applied for six cards meant that six companies were all searching her credit report at about the same time. To the organisations looking at later searches, she looked desperate for credit. They could assume she was in trouble and trying to borrow money quickly. They could assume that someone had stolen her identity and was trying to cash in quick. Either way, too many searches in a short space of time made the credit organisations nervous.

brilliant tip

When shopping around for the best deal, ask for a quotation rather than apply for credit. When the lender confirms that you can have the credit at the best deal, then you can finally apply. If the lender makes a quotation search, this does not leave a visible mark on your report for other lenders to see.

I am so organised that if you make a mistake I will get you to fix it pronto

There are a couple of reasons why you should check your own credit report.

- It is helpful to know what the organisation will see when they take the decision on whether or not to give you credit.
- Your credit report is an instant revelation if you have been the victim of identity theft.

How do I get a copy of my credit report?

- Write to each of the credit reference agencies enclosing a cheque for £2 and ask for your report to be sent to you.
- You can access your report through the website of each of the credit reference agencies. There is the opportunity to see your personal credit report for free by signing up to an online account with a free period of access. However, you must enter debit or credit card information and you will be charged a monthly fee if you have not cancelled the account before the end of the free access period.

What am I looking for?

Once you have a copy of your credit report, you need to check:

- Do only your addresses appear on the report?
- Are any people listed as associated with you correct?
- Do you recognise all the credit agreements shown?
- If there are late payments or missed payments shown, do you agree with the history?
- How many searches have been recorded lately? Are they all related to applications you have put forward?
- Are there any court judgments shown that you did not know about?

What if the information on my report is wrong?

You have the right to dispute any information you believe is wrong. You need to contact the organisation that gave you credit – not the credit agency – get them to agree the error and put it right. They should do this within 28 days. If they don't, you can then go to each credit agency and ask them to review your file or post a notice on your behalf on your file explaining the situation.

What if I think someone has stolen my identity?

If you have been the victim of identity theft, contact all the credit agencies, obtain your credit report and ask them to put an alert on your file. You may then need to involve the police.

If you are particularly worried about fraud and identity theft then you can pay for *protective registration*.

 **definition**

Protective registration

This places a warning against your address so that anyone carrying out a credit search will ask for more proof of identification before giving credit or granting a loan. The company may call or write to you to confirm that you have actually applied for credit. They may ask that you present your passport or some other form of photo ID before the application is approved.

Increasing your credit score

Before we move on to the third result a money lender looks for, let's quickly recap how you can begin to score the highest points in the credit score game:

- Don't move too often.
- Register to vote as soon as you move.
- Understand the terms and keep to them.
- Have some history of being able to pay for credit on time, all the time.
- Don't have more credit than you need.
- Make sure your credit report is correct.

Got that? Great – now on to the third and final result!

Result 3: If the person does not pay you back, you have another way of getting your money

How often have you seen adverts that start off 'If you are a home owner'? There is a reason for this, and it is an obvious one. If you have something of value and you don't pay your debts, then there is a chance that the lender can take you to court and seize something you own and sell it to recover their money.

If you are a homeowner, it is assumed that you also own other sellable items. This makes you a lower risk than someone who does not own a home. Some lenders even go as far as asking to have the debt secured against your home or other property. This then gives them the legal right to have the money paid back from the sale of that property before anyone else has a claim on the money.

🔍 brilliant recap

This chapter has introduced you to the idea of reviewing and understanding the information held by credit reference agencies. It explained how this information is used when you apply for credit.

Organisations who provide credit review your financial health by using reports from credit agencies.

- There are three main credit agencies in the UK: Equifax, Experian Callcredit.
- Other people's financial behaviour matters if you are financially linked to them.
- There are no credit blacklists.
- No debt can be worse than some debt.
- You can apply for credit too often.
- Your bad payment history is kept for six years.
- Registering to vote matters. ▶

- Public record information is shown on your file.

- You have a credit score on file.

If you have a bad credit history, you can work towards improving your situation:

- Check your report for errors and contact the creditor and have them fixed.

- Start to build up a good credit history by making sure the minimum balance is paid by direct debit.

- When searching for the best deal, ask for credit quotations rather than making a full application.

- Don't go for the best deals: you are most likely to be turned down and then have a search record on your credit report.

And finally . . .

Knowing your credit score and understanding your credit report is only useful if it helps you get where you want to go. Before you move to the next chapter, review your goals from Chapter 2 and make a note of possible actions on your to-do list related to your credit report that will take you closer to your goal.

Your net worth: what it means and why it is important

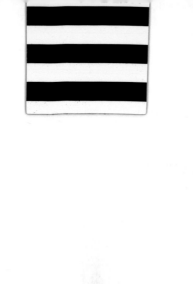

CHAPTER 6

Your net worth: what it means and why it is important

Risk comes from not knowing what you're doing.
                                    Warren Buffet, American investor

N et worth is the value of all your debts (the money you
owe) taken away from the realistic value of all the things
you own that could be sold and turned into cash.

The point of knowing your net worth

Think back to your comments in Chapter 2 relating to how you
worry about money. Most of us like to feel some sense of security.
In general, it is quite difficult – and some would say impossible –
to get through life without having debts of some description. But
debt, if managed well, can be used to achieve your goals without
causing stress and anxiety. Using the net worth tool in this
chapter will allow you to keep your debt in perspective and keep
it from becoming a problem. It will ensure you have all the information you need to make the right financial choices, either on
your own or with the help of a financial adviser.

brilliant example

Peter has been worrying about the level of their household debt. This
month the bills and credit card statements seem to be larger than normal.
He thinks that they must be close to being bankrupt! He feels sure that   ▶

even if they sell everything they own, they will still have a large amount of outstanding debt.

His best friend tells him not to worry but instead take action. Together, they realistically value all the household possessions and take away the total value of the household debts. When Peter sees the result, he realises that, although the debt is high, if he had to he could pay his debts in full and still have money left over.

Peter may be right to feel that the household debt is too high. However, understanding his net worth will allow him to judge whether or not the level of debt is out of control. If he matches the result of his net worth calculation with his life and financial goals he can use the detail to plan changes in how he manages and structures his finances.

Calculating your net worth

Use Table 6.1 to help you calculate your net worth. The table has two sides: one side for all the things you own and one side for all your debts. You need to complete the table by filling in the amounts currently relevant to you. Remember, if you are not at home with the numbers at your fingertips, then complete the table with a close guess and then compare to reality later.

When you have filled in the relevant amounts in each column, add up the columns to get Totals 1 and 2. Then work out your net worth by taking Total 2 away from Total 1.

brilliant tip

To find the actual amounts for Table 6.1:

● Check your latest statements for bank, loans, store cards, credit cards, mortgage, catalogue, pensions and savings.

▶

Table 6.1 Net worth

Things owned by me/us	Amount	Things owed by me/us	Amount
Cash		Mortgage	
Bank accounts		Credit cards	
ISAs		Bank loans	
Endowment insurance/savings plan		Bank overdraft	
Pension plan		Store cards	
Property		Hire purchase	
Shares		Student loan	
Cars		Catalogue	
Jewellery		Friends and family	
Antiques/art/collectables		Unpaid tax	
Other equipment		Other bills	
Other		Other	
TOTAL 1		TOTAL 2	

My/our net worth (Total 1 minus Total 2) = £

- To value your property realistically, check your local
  paper for the selling price of similar properties or go to
  www.nethouseprices.com for the land registry record of sales in
  your area.
- Use the valuation on your insurance documents for any insured
  possessions.
- Go to your local trader magazine or website to check the
  advertised prices for uninsured possessions.

What does your net worth mean?

If the value of the things you own is higher than the debts you have

You have a positive net worth. Overall, if you have to, you could pay off all your debts right now and still have money left over. Hopefully that is a situation you will not be forced into. If you worry about having debt, then this result should make you feel a little better. The next job is deciding whether or not the amount left over is actually large enough to support your life and financial goals.

If the value of the things you own is lower than the debts you have

This means that your net worth is negative. If everyone that you owed money to wanted their payment right now, not all of them would go away happy. Provided you make all your payments on time and don't keep adding to your debt, then this will change over time. Whether you worry about this situation or not will depend on your life and financial goals. The two following situations are completely different and show how sometimes negative net worth is a necessity.

Situation 1

A young student has a student loan and no property. They have a negative net worth. However, their life goal at the moment is to get a degree so that they can enter the career of their choice. The structure of the student loan means that they will not have someone knocking on their door for the money until they are actually in a position to pay the money back. So in this situation having a negative net worth is a necessity and not a great risk.

Situation 2

A young couple with a newborn baby have a 100% mortgage on their home. The value of their house is equal to the mortgage debt. They have credit card debts of £5,000 and a £1,000 loan for the car. They have a negative net worth. They are not in a position to repay all of their debt at once. Having a negative net worth means that it will be highly important that they keep to their agreements and make all their debt payments on time. Missing payments and falling far behind in payments may mean that their credit agreements are cancelled and they may be asked to repay the money borrowed before they can afford to. Over time, their net worth may move to a positive position if the value of their house goes up and their debts reduce.

Knowing whether or not you have a positive or negative net worth will help you put debts into perspective. It will also help you see whether you are reaching your goals. You may, for instance, have a long-term goal to be debt-free and have enough of a nest egg to retire early. With the help of a financial adviser you can determine what your net worth needs to be and in which category your money should be in order to achieve your goal.

By completing Table 6.1 you now have a list that you can use as we move on to look at money products and how you can make choices and develop a plan of action. The next two chapters will help you with this.

↗ brilliant recap

- Net worth is the value of your debts taken away from the value of things you own.

- Knowing your net worth will help your financial adviser provide the best advice for your situation.

- Negative net worth is not necessarily bad if you have a plan to clear your debts and if it meets your needs.

- Knowing and understanding your net worth puts your debt in perspective.

CHAPTER 7

Reviewing your financial choices – Part 1

Bank accounts, interest rates, savings, pensions and property

Before you spend, earn. Before you invest, investigate.
William A. Ward, American writer and teacher

You are beginning to put together your own personal finance portfolio. However, having all this information about your finances is only useful if you use it to improve your situation.

At the end of Chapter 2 we recommended that you made a note of your goals and rewards and put them somewhere you could see them every day. You now need to refer to them while you work through the rest of this chapter. This is because decisions affecting your financial situation should always be taken within the context of your financial and life goals.

The aim of this chapter and the next is to help you make a list of areas where you can, or need to, take some action to improve your financial situation – all within the context of your goals. Remember that something that makes financial sense may not always take you towards your goal. As you read through each section, make notes on your Action list (Table 1.1) of any relevant actions suggested or that occur to you.

 **example**

This year at Suzanne's birthday dinner her grandmother gave her a cheque for £1,000 with a note saying 'Just an advance on your inheritance so that you can see a bit of the world'. Suzanne could not believe it. Her father told her that if she put the £1,000 into a high-interest savings account for three years, she would have more money available for travelling. She could also add extra savings to the account each month. Suzanne agreed that if she could save, add to the money and lock it away for three years then that would be a sensible option. But that was much further in the future than her original goal. Suzanne's financial personality meant that she would *never* add a great deal to her grandmother's money and would probably find a reason to dip into it. She finally decided to use the money as intended to travel, but would do her research and get the best travelling deal she could.

For Suzanne, travelling is her goal; saving and being secure is not. She made her decision not based on the best potential financial outcome, but on how she wants to live her life. Sometimes it's not about making more money but being smart about living the life you want with the money you have. Remember this as you put together your action points.

The net worth categories and how the money products work

As we look at each net worth category, it makes sense to explain how the relevant money products work and any options available to you when trying to work out your plan of action for the future.

Money in the bank and savings

What is the difference between a bank and a building society?

- **A building society** is a money club with membership. It is just like the golf society or the music society except that this is a society that looks after money. The members of the society choose directors to run the organisation and all the members benefit if they make a profit. There are no shareholders, just the people who use the society for their savings, loans or mortgages. Building societies must get more than 50% of the money they lend out in mortgages and loans from the cash saved by their members. The rest they can borrow from other money institutions. This generally makes them a lower-risk organisation.

- **A bank** is a company whose shares are often available to be bought and sold on the stock market. The shareholders choose directors to run the organisation and require a profit in return for their investment. This means that not all the profit made will benefit the savers or borrowers who have accounts with the bank. Some profit is given to the shareholders. Banks can raise the money for their loans and mortgages from the shareholders, savers and other money institutions.

How interest rates work

We have already discovered that when you borrow money the lender requires a reward for the risk taken. This is in the form of interest. Equally, when you deposit money with a bank or building society they will give you a reward for using your money. The reward they give you will be based on the risk you take, the commitment given and how much they need or want your money.

The calculation of interest can be quite complicated. Interest may be calculated daily, monthly, quarterly or annually. The following situations use the simple annual calculation to explain how interest works when you deposit money with a bank or building society.

Situation 1

You have deposited £1,000 into a savings account. The agreement is that you do not take the money out for 12 months and your reward will be 5% interest. At the end of the 12 months your reward calculation is:

$$£1,000 \times 5\% = £50$$

If you take out all your money at the end of 12 months, you will have £1,050 in your pocket.

Situation 2

You have the same £1,000 and the same 5% interest reward. You decide to leave your money in the account for two years. You take your reward out of the account at the end of each year and spend it. Your reward calculation is:

$$\text{End of year 1: } £1,000 \times 5\% = £50$$

$$\text{End of year 2: } £1,000 \times 5\% = £50$$

You have received £100 in reward in total over two years, and your money back.

Situation 3

You have the same £1,000 and the same 5% interest reward. This time you decide not to take your reward at the end of each year but leave it in the account with the original £1,000. Your reward calculation is:

$$\text{End of year 1: } £1,000 \times 5\% = 50$$
(your new account balance is now £1,050)

$$\text{End of year 2: } £1,050 \times 5\% = £52.50$$
(your account balance is now £1,102.50)

You have received £102.50 reward and your money back.

Considerations

This last situation uses *compounding*. You receive interest on your interest as well as the original deposit. An extra £2.50 does not sound like much of an extra reward. However, this is only over two years. Compounding is much more useful when used over longer periods as a way of creating more money for a specific event or future plan.

In our case study, Rob and Andrew want to establish their independence but also plan for a comfortable future. If they were to do something simple they could put £1,000 into an account for 20 years; choosing an account that provides 5% interest every year, added to their balance automatically. When they come back to the account 20 years later, they would have £2,653.30: their original £1,000 and interest of £1,653.30. Again, this may not seem like a great deal of money.

To make the reward more interesting, instead of just putting a lump sum of money away and forgetting about it, they could regularly add to their account, say £1,000 each year. They would then have saved £20,000 and would receive

> compounding and regular saving can produce the lump sum you need for that future event

£14,719.25 in reward: a total of £34,719.25. To keep these examples simple, it is assumed that there is no tax to pay on the interest received. Obviously the more you save and the higher the interest rate, the bigger the reward. So, compounding and regular saving can produce the lump sum you need for that future event.

Table 7.1 shows how different interest rates will produce different rewards for Rob and Andrew.

Table 7.1 Interest rate rewards

Interest rate	5%	6%	7%
Total interest reward	£14,719	£18,992	£23,865
Total saved over 20 years	£20,000	£20,000	£20,000
Amount in account at the end	£34,719	£38,992	£43,865
Percentage return on savings	73%	94%	119%

Hopefully you get the idea. Using compounding with regular savings means that you get a higher return for your money. Don't worry – you don't have to work this all out for yourself. There are a number of online calculators that will tell you how much to expect from your money. You just need to know how long you want to save for and what interest rates are available.

Here is another example from our case studies.

 **example**

Peter is thinking about starting a family and all the expense that is involved. One of the expenses on his mind is the cost of education. By using the idea of regularly saving a relatively small amount each month, and the principle of compounding, Peter can have a lump sum available when his child is 18 and ready to go to university.

Types of account

Now that you understand the difference between building societies and banks and the reward you can receive from saving, we will take a look at the different types of accounts available to you.

Basic bank account

This is a no 'credit check' account. It is ideal if you think you would fail a credit check because you have a bad credit history or were once bankrupt but are now discharged. Even people with a bad credit history can still have a basic bank account. You just need to prove who you are. You get a *cash card* and can set up *standing orders* and *direct debits*. You will not be able to go overdrawn and the fees for breaking the rules will be higher than other types of account.

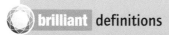 **definitions**

Cash card

A plastic card that you can use to withdraw cash from the bank or ATM (automatic teller machine – often called 'hole in the wall').

Standing order

An instruction to the bank to make a specific payment to someone on a regular basis.

Direct debit

When someone takes regular payments from your account with your permission.

Savings/deposit account

This account will pay you to keep your money in it. You are now renting your money to the bank or building society and they pay you interest on the amount you have given them. You will have a passbook or savings account card to use when you deposit or withdraw your money. You cannot set up standing orders or direct debits with this account: it is meant for saving, not daily transactions.

Current account

To open this type of account you will need to pass a credit check. You can have a cash card, *debit card*, *guarantee card*, set up direct debits and standing orders, have a *cheque book* and possibly an *overdraft facility*.

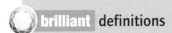 **definitions**

Debit card

A plastic card that you can use to pay for goods. The money is taken from your bank account immediately: it is a plastic form of cash.

Cheque book

A book of paper where you write the amount you want the bank to pay to the person whose name you have put at the top. The person you give the cheque to must give it to their bank, so that the bank can request the money to be transferred to that person's own account.

Guarantee card

A card that goes with the cheque book. The person you give the cheque to can quote the number of your card and this will guarantee that the money is transferred from your account to theirs even if you don't have enough money in your account. The card usually has a limit of £50 or £100.

Overdraft facility

Where the bank lets you spend more than you have in your account. You will then be charged interest and possibly a fee for using their money.

e-savings account

This is a bank account that you can only see online using the internet. It is a type of savings account that is connected to your current account and will normally pay a higher interest rate than an ordinary current account. You can only transfer money between the e-savings account and your other accounts, using the internet.

Offset account

This is a savings account that is usually only available online and must be operated through your mortgage provider. It does not pay interest on the balance but saves you interest on your mortgage. It is not part of your mortgage but attached to your mortgage in such a way that the balance is used to calculate the interest you need to pay on your mortgage. For example, on interest calculation day the amount shown as owing on your mortgage could be £100,000. The mortgage company would then use this balance to calculate the interest you must pay. If you had £10,000 in the attached offset account, then the amount used for calculating the interest charge would be £90,000.

All-in-one account

This is an account that behaves like a current account with a large overdraft. You can use it like a current account. You can have your salary paid into it and all your bills paid out of it. You can have a cheque book and debit card to use with the account. The overdraft is actually a mortgage. Interest is normally charged based on the daily balance, so as you have money paid into the account and the overdraft reduces, you pay less in interest. If you keep within the agreed limit then there are no extra charges. Some accounts only require that you have cleared the agreed overdraft facility by the time you retire.

Using online banking

This is where you access your bank account details using the internet rather than going to the bank. You will need passwords and extra personal identification numbers (PIN) to keep your details secure. You can print statements, transfer money, set up payments, ask for an overdraft, or set up standing orders. If your account is online only, then any cheques or cash you want to pay into the account will have to be sent by post to a central processing office.

Making decisions about cash and money in the bank

Situation 1

You constantly have a reasonably large balance in a bank account or building society account that is earning little or no interest. You need to feel that there are funds instantly available for an emergency.

Possible actions

You can take a number of actions to improve the situation without being unable to access your money if you need it. Many of us just leave our money in one account because it is the account we opened when we first started working.

> many of us just leave our money in one account because it is the account we opened when we first started working

If you have a mortgage, check if your mortgage provider offers an offset account facility with the mortgage. If you move your savings to the offset account, it can be used to reduce the overall balance due and the interest charged. The money will still be available to withdraw if you need it.

Another action to consider is finding a higher interest savings account and, if you have not used all your allowance, one that is an *ISA* and also allows you instant access to your money if you need it. Then you can transfer the surplus money from your current account to this new ISA savings account.

brilliant definition

ISA

Individual savings account: a savings plan that meets criteria
approved by the UK Government and allows you to have the profit
without paying tax on it. You have a limit on the amount you can
place in your ISA each tax year (the tax year runs from 6 April to
5 April the next year). From 6 April 2010 the total investment
allowed is £10,200, with only £5,100 allowed as a cash savings
account; the rest must be invested in a stocks-and-shares based
savings plan.

The way to decide which action is the right one is to compare
which one will either save the most money per pound or provide
the most reward per pound.

brilliant example

- £1 in a current account with no interest pays £0 reward.
- £1 in an ISA account giving 6% interest per year pays 6p per year (tax-free).
- £1 in an offset account against a mortgage costing 5% saves 5p per year.

Situation 2

You constantly have a reasonably large balance in a bank
account or building society account that is earning little or no
interest. You never really look at your account and do not realise
that the balance never goes below a certain amount. You do not
feel the need to keep some emergency money available.

Possible actions

In this situation it will help to look at the debt side of your net worth table (see page 87). If you find that you have credit or store card balances and are not paying them off in full each month then using the surplus money to clear the debt is an option. Alternatively, if you have a mortgage that allows you to make additional repayments, you could use the money to reduce your outstanding mortgage debt.

At this point you may be looking at the net worth table and wondering how to make the best use of surplus money when you have outstanding debts. The simple answer is to put the debts in order of expense and pay off the debt that costs you the most or saves you the most money by paying it off.

pay off the debt that costs you the most

 **brilliant** example

Suzanne's brother, Sean, has over £1,000 constantly in his current bank account. The interest he receives once a year is based on 0.1% of the average balance. He has no particular reason for keeping this amount in the bank. He also has a store card with an average outstanding balance of £800, and a credit card with an average outstanding balance of £700. He decides that he does not need to keep the £1,000 in the bank and should pay off his debts since every month they are costing him money in interest payments. He writes down the following figures:

	Bank	Store card	Credit card
Interest rate charged or received per year	0.1%	29%	17%
Average balance	£1,000	£800	£700
Annual interest estimated	£1 received	£232 paid	£119 paid

He decides to pay his store card balance in full. He realises that this balance is costing him the most in interest. He then decides to pay £200 towards his credit card bill.

Endowment insurance policies

Many people have used an endowment policy as a vehicle to save the amount of money needed to pay off the balance of their mortgage at the end of its term. It used to be common for mortgage brokers to sell an interest-only mortgage along with an endowment policy, assuring the purchaser that in the long term the mortgage could be paid with the proceeds from the policy.

 brilliant definition

Endowment insurance

A type of life insurance. The insured person pays a monthly premium to the insurance company for an agreed length of time (typically 20–25 years). The insurance company invests the money paid to them, less their fee. At the end of the time period (the policy maturity date), the value of the life insurance is paid to the insured person (if they are still alive).

Making decisions about savings plans

Here is an example that highlights the decisions you need to make about savings plans.

The situation

You do not have a savings plan. Your savings amount to whatever is left over each month from your salary. However, you have a specific event in the long-term future that you know you have to pay for.

Possible actions

1 Do nothing and borrow the money you need in the future.

2 Work out how much money you will need in the future and

exactly when. Talk to an expert about the potential, guaranteed reward savings plans. Find out how much you would need to save and invest per month to achieve the minimum amount you need. Then find a way of saving it.

Option 1 is really only possible if there is no way of finding the money to save from now until the day you need the money. Although it does beg the question, if you can't find the monthly amount now, how will you find more later to pay for the amount you have to borrow? How do you know that anyone will lend it to you when you need it?

Let's compare the two options. We will assume you need £20,000 and the interest rate for both options is 5% after tax is considered, and you need the £20,000 in 10 years' time.

- Saving £1,408 per year will give you a balance of just over £20,000 at the end of 10 years and will only cost you £14,080.

- Borrowing £20,000 at 5% interest charged and making the same monthly payments would take 25 years to pay off and a total of £35,732.

By planning ahead and choosing the right savings plan you can save yourself £21,652. Even if you were able to borrow the money at 0% interest then it would still cost £5,922 more to borrow than to have a savings plan.

brilliant tip

When deciding whether to save or borrow, take the total amount to be paid back from borrowing less the amount you would need to pay into a savings plan. This would be the extra cost of borrowing. Think about what you could do with that money if you did not have to pay it to the money lender.

Before moving to the next category, take a moment to consider if a savings plan could help you achieve your longer-term goals.

Making decisions about pension plans

A *pension plan* is a long-term savings plan that is given tax-free status by the Government so long as it meets specific criteria. If you are a taxpayer, the Government contributes the tax already paid on the money you contribute to an approved pension scheme. The Government also allows your employer to contribute tax-free money to a company pension scheme on your behalf. There are rules that limit how much you can contribute tax-free each year and in the whole of your lifetime.

Currently you are allowed to access the pension savings from the age of 55 to 75. Under the rules in place at the time of printing, 25% can be taken as a lump sum payment and 75% of the money must be used to buy an annuity. An annuity is a product that allows you to pay a lump sum to an organisation that in return provides a guaranteed monthly income for the rest of your life.

We are not going to spend time here going through the complicated world of pensions and the rules surrounding how they are managed. But it is worth remembering that the rules of compounding work here. The earlier you contribute to a pension plan, the more you get for your money in the end.

One of the most frequent questions I am asked is: 'Do I really need a private or company pension plan?' The Government and pension provider would always say 'Yes'!

However, this book is about giving you the basis for a decision, not the answer. Consider these questions in your quest to decide whether or not you need to think about contributing towards a pension plan:

Ⓠ **Can you imagine a time in your life when you will not go to work to earn a living?**

Ⓐ The majority of people say 'Yes'.

Ⓠ **If you agree that you will not always work to provide an income, how much income will you need to live a decent life when you retire?**

Ⓐ The answer to this one will depend on how old you are and what you want to do when you retire. If you are in your twenties or even younger, don't skip this part. Just because you think that retiring is a long time away, it does not mean you should not start preparing for it now.

Ⓠ **Can you guarantee that you will have that income when you need it?**

Ⓐ Generally the answer to this question is 'No' or 'I don't know'. If your answer is one of these two, then add two things to your to-do list:

● Think about and estimate the income I need when I retire.

● Find out how much I would need to invest to generate the income needed.

If you have not thought too much about investing in a pension or creating extra income for when you retire, try living a couple of weeks on the weekly current state pension and see what sort of lifestyle it will allow you. This will certainly help you decide if you need to make some provision for later in life.

> try living a couple of weeks on the weekly current state pension and see what sort of lifestyle it will allow you

brilliant tip

If you have been working and paying your national insurance in the UK, then every couple of years you should ask the Pension Service, part of the Department for Work and Pensions, for a forecast of the state pension you will receive when you retire. You can do this online at www.direct.gov.uk, under the heading 'Money, tax and benefits'. This will give you a starting point to working out the extra income you may need when you retire.

Most people think that money invested in a pension scheme must be linked to the stock market. This may put off those people who do not like to take risks with their money. But your pension savings plan does not have to be invested in stocks and shares. You can invest in property, or you can choose very safe cash-based investments. The disadvantage of a very safe or low-risk investment is that it may take longer to accumulate the amount of savings you need: alternatively you may need to invest more on a regular basis. This is an area where you do need the help of a suitably qualified financial adviser.

Reviewing the value of your property

When looking at the value of your property in the net worth table, it is important to establish the reason for owning the property.

Situation 1
The property is your home and primarily for the pleasure of living rather than making a profit.

Considerations
Most people say they need to feel their home is safe and will not be taken from them. To see how safe you are, take the value of

your property and compare it to the amount of money you owe on your mortgage. The first safe sign is that the mortgage balance owing is less than the value of the house. This will mean that, unless you break your agreement with the mortgage provider, there is no reason for them to change the payment arrangement. If the value of the mortgage is higher than the value of the house, it means you are in *negative equity*. Consider actively thinking about ways to reduce the mortgage balance to bring you to a safer position.

it is always cheaper to keep things regularly maintained

Unless your goal is to make a profit on your home, then one of your aims should be to maintain its value. Do this by keeping every part of the home maintained. It is always cheaper to keep things regularly maintained rather than letting them run down and then having to pay for major repairs or redecoration.

Situation 2
The property is held for rental income or profit.

Considerations
Keeping track of the value of this property versus the mortgage balance is also important. There are lots of advantages and tax implications relating to owning this type of property. Always take expert advice about your plans and situation to make sure you make the most profit from your investment. Always have the expected reward in mind. Although this book is not about investing, remember that money is a tool and you always need to know what you want from it to be able to take critical decisions at the right time.

Reviewing your shares

People accumulate *shares* for all kinds of different reasons. Some shares may have been inherited, some may have been received as part of their membership of a building society that is now a bank, or maybe the shares were just purchased because they looked like a good investment. When looking at this category in your net worth table, ask yourself some questions.

● Why do you hold these shares?

● What reward do you want from them?

We go back to the same core action point. Take a look at your investment in shares in the overall context of your goals. Will they help you achieve your short-term or long-term goals?

brilliant tip

If you plan to keep a relatively large value of shares and reinvest your dividend payments for when you retire, then find out if these shares can be wrapped in a pension plan. This way, you will accumulate a pension fund with some tax relief from the Government. This will depend on your circumstances and whether or not the cost of setting up the pension is more than the tax saving.

Your possessions: cars, antiques and other stuff

When we get to this category in a personal finance workshop most people underestimate the value of their possessions. Take a really good look at everything you own – the remaining items on the left-hand side of your net worth table. They will fall into two categories.

1　Valuable.

2　Not so valuable or worthless.

On the valuable list, your first concern is to make sure that the items are adequately insured. But insurance aside, you also might want to consider the purpose of owning each item. If the reason is sentimental, then possibly that is the end of it. If you don't really have a reason, then again refer back to your goals. See if those possessions can be put to some good use.

On the not-so-valuable or worthless list there will be some items that you really should just get rid of. But don't just throw things away. The items you don't need anymore could be useful to someone else. There are lots of free advertising opportunities out there, particularly on the internet.

brilliant example

When Peter and Helen last redecorated they bought two flat-screen televisions, one for the kitchen area and one for the main sitting room. The old televisions they had in each room still worked perfectly well. They had been sitting in one of the bedrooms waiting for Peter to take them to the council refuse dump. After looking at his net worth calculation, Peter decided to try and sell the televisions instead of dumping them. He took a photo of each television and advertised them locally on the internet. Within two weeks he had sold both of them to students. The students were moving away from home for the first time and didn't have a great deal of money. Peter made £50 and used this towards paying off one of the store cards on his debt list.

↗ brilliant recap

Savings and investments are a good thing. To make the best use of them, remember:

- Compound interest with regular savings provides faster growth in your pot of money.
- ISAs are useful tax-free savings plans.
- The earlier you plan for your pension, the cheaper it is to create a large pot of money for your retirement.
- You can get a pension forecast from www.direct.gov.uk.
- Never extend your mortgage to create savings, as the interest paid on the mortgage will generally cost more than the return on your savings investment.

Now that we have reviewed the left-hand side of the net worth table, we can move on to the right-hand side and review your level of debt.

CHAPTER 8

Reviewing your financial choices – Part 2

Mortgages, credit cards, loans and overdrafts

He who does not economise will have to agonise.

Confucius, Chinese philosopher

I n this chapter we will use the right-hand side of your net worth table to guide us through the potential debts that you may have or may be planning to accumulate to support your goals. Remember, debt is not a bad thing if managed correctly with a specific reward in mind.

All about mortgages

A *mortgage* is a secured loan. This means that you borrow money from an organisation to buy a property. This lender has the right to take the property from you if for some reason you are unable to keep your agreement and pay back the debt.

What is involved in getting a mortgage?

- When you apply for a mortgage the lender will perform a credit check to see if you are low enough risk to deal with.

- You will need to prove that you have enough income to be able to pay back the loan in monthly instalments, or that you have a savings plan in place to pay back the loan at the end of the agreed term.

- You will have to make sure that the property is insured. If something happens to the house, the insurance will pay for the house to be repaired or rebuilt.

● The lender will want an independent valuation of the property to make sure that if they need to take the property instead of the money, it is actually worth more than the amount borrowed.

There you have it, the basics. A mortgage is essentially just a big loan. The different names given to a mortgage just describe how the mortgage is to be repaid or how the interest amount is calculated.

Types of mortgage

There are two ways of paying back a mortgage loan: *repayment* or *interest only*.

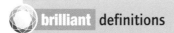 **brilliant** definitions

Interest-only mortgage

A loan for a specific amount and period of time borrowed from a mortgage provider to buy a property. If the loan is not paid back at the end of the period, the mortgage provider can repossess the property in order to obtain the amount owed. Over the period agreed, the borrower pays an agreed amount of monthly interest but nothing towards paying back the amount borrowed; the full amount is then paid back at the end of the time period. The borrower effectively rents the money until it is time to pay it back.

Repayment mortgage

Where you borrow an amount of money to buy a property. Every month you pay back some of the borrowed amount and some of the interest payable. At the end of the agreed term the whole amount has been repaid.

There are many ways of calculating the interest rate attached to a mortgage but the two basics are *fixed* and *variable*:

- **Fixed**: The interest rate is agreed in advance and does not change until the agreed specific date.
- **Variable**: The interest rate goes up and down depending on the Bank of England base rate.

 brilliant definition

Bank of England base rate

The Bank of England will lend money to other banking institutions. Like all money lenders, it will want a reward for its trouble. It will charge interest at a set rate, which is reviewed every month.

The mortgage provider obtains the money they lend to you from someone else. This can be a saver, the Bank of England, or another organisation. The mortgage provider will have to pay a reward for using that money. The reward is interest. The mortgage provider will then want their own reward on top for lending the money to you.

Let's look at a really simple example:

- X Bank agrees to lend you £50,000.
- X Bank borrows from the Bank of England £50,000.
- X Bank pays 0.5% interest to the Bank of England.
- X Bank adds 3% interest for its own reward.
- You are charged 3.5% standard variable interest as part of your mortgage.

Note that the mortgage provider can change its reward percentage at any time: that part is not linked to the Bank of England interest rate.

If your agreement is for a *tracker* variable interest rate mortgage, then when the Bank of England puts its rate up then your rate will go up too.

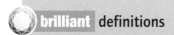 **definitions**

Tracker interest rate mortgage

Where the mortgage company agrees to charge a specific percentage rate above the Bank of England interest rate.

Discounted variable interest rate mortgage

Where the mortgage company agrees to reduce their standard variable rate by a specific percentage for a period of time. This means that if the organisation's variable rate goes up then your interest rate goes up, if their standard variable rate goes down then your interest rate goes down.

Remember always that the aim of the mortgage provider is to make a profit on the agreement.

Making decisions about mortgages

Now that you understand the basics of a mortgage loan, you can make decisions about your net worth and future plans. For instance, you may have a goal to be debt free as fast as possible so that you can use the money you pay to a mortgage for something else in life.

> reduce the amount you have borrowed as fast as you can

The key actions are to obtain the lowest interest rate you can and reduce the amount you have borrowed as fast as you can. Using an online simple mortgage calculator you make the kind of comparisons shown in Table 8.1.

Table 8.1 Mortgage calculations

Assumed interest rate	Total interest paid		Monthly payments expected	
	Over 20 years	Over 25 years	Over 20 years	Over 25 years
3.5%	78,380	100,375	1,160	1,001
4%	90,870	116,701	1,213	1,056
5%	116,778	150,754	1,320	1,169

Mortgage amount: £200,000
Type of mortgage: repayment

The higher the interest and the longer the term, the more you are paying for the privilege of borrowing the money. This may be unavoidable when you first take out a mortgage, but that does not mean that you have to stick with the same arrangement for 20 or 25 years.

Many people have agreed to a 20-year mortgage term. I hear people say 'Our mortgage will be finished in 20XX and then we will be able to do X and Y'. When I ask them whether it could be finished earlier so that they could do X and Y while they are still young, they often give me a strange look and say 'How can we do that?' The answer depends on whether or not you can make more money available either in lump sums occasionally or on a regular monthly basis.

 **example**

Suzanne's parents had a repayment mortgage which still had seven years to go before it was paid off. Their outgoings were lower than they used to be and so they found they had more money left over each month. They would very much like to travel a bit more before they get too old. Suzanne's mum called their mortgage provider and asked if there was a way they   ▶

could pay off the mortgage more quickly. The provider asked her if they could make higher payments each month. She gave them a figure of how much more they could now afford to pay. The adviser calculated that if they increased their monthly payments they would have paid the rest of the mortgage off in three years.

If this is something that fits with your goals, then the key information you need from your mortgage provider is:

● Can you make extra payments to reduce the amount of the mortgage without incurring extra penalties?

● Will your mortgage provider let you have a better deal as a current customer without having to go through the whole process of reapplying for a new mortgage?

Again, let's look at some numbers using a popular online calculator:

● Mortgage amount £200,000.

● Agreed term 20 years.

● Agreed interest rate 3.5%.

● If the borrower overpays each month by £200, the mortgage will be paid off four years earlier than planned.

brilliant tip

When you get a pay rise or have a financial windfall that was not expected – and before you spend it all on a one-off item – look at what the impact would be on your future if that money was put towards reducing the time you have to pay off a debt.

Our final example highlights the costly decisions that can be made when using mortgages and loans to finance your life.

 **example**

When Peter and Helen last moved house they also remortgaged. The amount they needed for the mortgage was £50,000 less than the value of the house. They decided to apply for £25,000 more than they needed to buy the house. They used £15,000 to buy a car and put £10,000 in their savings account for a rainy day. The mortgage was to be paid back over 20 years at an interest rate of 5%.

The extra £25,000 will cost them £8,758 in interest payments. Even if they are able to invest the £10,000 at 5% in their savings account, they will still have to pay tax on that interest. This means that their savings are actually costing them money. In addition they will probably still be paying for the car long after they need to change it for a new one.

What would have been a more sensible decision for Peter and Helen, if they still felt they needed a car and savings?

- Obtain the mortgage amount they originally needed.
- Finance the car with a short-term loan or 0% finance deal instead, matching the time period spent paying for the car with its useful life.
- Put the amount saved on monthly mortgage repayments into a high-interest tax-free savings plan every month to build up a nest egg.

Endowment policies

Finally, let's look at a problem associated with mortgages that may affect you.

The situation

You have an endowment policy and are depending on this policy to repay your mortgage. The last forecast received from the provider of the endowment policy shows that it will not be enough to pay the full mortgage amount that will be due at the end of the term. You have not thought of checking if the policy was mis-sold.

Possible actions

There has been much publicity surrounding the potential mis-selling of endowment policies in the past. Many people have received compensation, if their claim that their policy was mis-sold was accepted, helping them to bridge the gap between the mortgage repayment and the amount to be received from the endowment policy. The time limit for making a claim may have passed, but it is still worth investigating the possibility of making a claim against the company who sold the policy.

> ⭐ **brilliant** tip
>
> If you are not sure if your endowment policy was mis-sold, then go to www.which.co.uk/advice/mis-sold-endowments-how-to-claim or contact your local Citizens Advice Bureau for more advice.

Choosing products wisely

An endowment insurance policy in itself is not a bad product. It is just one kind of savings product that also provides life insurance. The negative attitude today surrounding the use of endowment policies as a way of saving to pay off your interest-only mortgage is because in the past some advisers were over-optimistic about the lump sum that would be available at the end of the savings plan. They did not explain clearly enough to the policy holder that there was a risk that the amount needed might not be available if the insurance company did not invest the premiums in a way that created enough return. It was the fact that people assumed the policy was guaranteed to give them the lump sum they needed that caused the investigation into mis-selling.

The key to using any savings plan to pay off a debt is to make sure you ask for the worst case scenario and use this as your basis for purchasing a money product.

Understanding credit cards

A *credit card* is just like money. It is a piece of plastic that you present and is a promise that the organisation who gave you the card will pay for the goods you want to buy. The key thing is that it is linked to an account that has been opened in your name.

A *credit card account* is an agreement between you and the credit card company that it will pay for your spending up to an agreed amount if you agree to pay it back and give the company a reward for the money it pays out on your behalf. You agree to its rules on how this should be done and if you don't keep to the rules the company can fine you, charge you extra or come and take its money back. There is nothing in the agreement that says this relationship is forever. The credit card company can change its decision and close your account, so long as it keeps to its own rules about how it does it.

How a credit card works

You are given a credit limit. This is the total amount of money you can owe to the credit card company at any one time. You buy the goods, the credit card company pays for them and then you pay the company later. If you try to spend more than your credit limit then your card will be refused. You are given an account number, which will be printed on the front of your card so you don't have to remember it. You will have a security code: three numbers on the back of the card next to your signature. These numbers relate specifically to you. You also have a PIN.

 **definition**

PIN

Personal identification number: a four-digit number that only you and the credit card company know. You will use this number to confirm you are allowed to use the card when buying something in person and processing your card through a machine. You will have agreed with the credit card company that you will not give this number to anyone or keep it written down.

Remember we said that borrowing money is like renting it. Credit card companies will generally give you a rent-free period (commonly known as interest free): an amount of time before they start charging interest. This will be anything from 16 to 46 days, depending on when in the month you make your purchase.

brilliant example

Suzanne used her credit card to buy a pair of shoes on 10 September. The credit card company put together her statement on 17 September and so adds her shoe purchase to the statement. She then had to pay her balance by 3 October if she did not want to be charged interest on the money. She had 23 days of interest-free money.

Suzanne then bought a new coat on 18 September and the credit card company added this purchase to her statement on 17 October and told her she needed to pay her balance by 2 November to avoid being charged interest on the money. This time she had 45 days of interest-free money.

Credit cards are designed to buy things with, not to withdraw cash. If you use the card to withdraw cash from the bank, or use it to pay for your lottery ticket (the credit card company counts this as cash) then there is no interest-free period. You start paying interest as soon as you receive the cash.

Using a credit card abroad

Most credit cards can be used abroad, but you should check with the credit card company to find out whether there are any extra charges each time you use the card.

What do VISA, Mastercard and AMEX mean?

These are the three major companies who actually provide the money that you spend using your plastic credit card. AMEX is the name for American Express. If you have an American Express Card then you have an agreement directly with American Express. It gives you the plastic card, sends you your statements and pays for the things you buy with your credit card.

If you have a plastic card that says VISA or Mastercard on it then things are a little different. A Barclays VISA card is managed by Barclays but the money to pay for your purchases comes from VISA. Barclays is the go-between selling you a VISA credit card. Mastercard works in exactly the same way. VISA and Mastercard never send out their own credit cards and you never pay anything directly to VISA or Mastercard.

Credit cards: what's the big deal?

All credit cards have a credit limit that you have to keep to. They are all designed to charge you interest if you don't pay all the outstanding amount shown on the due date. So, if you decide you are going to use a credit card, how can you choose which one to have? Like all products, you should buy the one that fits the purpose you want to use it for.

If you decide you need a new washing machine there are some features that you will think are important and some you don't really care about. If you have only a small space, then the size will matter. If you are big on energy efficiency, then the machine's energy rating will matter. If it is fitting into a specifically designed room, then the colour may matter. If you don't have much money, then maybe all of the above don't matter so long as the washing machine is cheap. It is the same with a credit card. You make your choice according to your needs.

Types of credit card

Here are the different types of card available at the time of publishing.

Standard credit card

On this card you are given a credit limit and an interest rate that is variable, plus standard fees if you break the rules and pay late.

0% balance transfer credit card

Designed for people who already have a balance on a credit card and are being charged interest on the balance, this card offers an extended period of interest at 0%. Generally the 0% interest period is anything from 6 to 16 months. You need to have a good credit score, so this card works for people who pay on time but have just built up a large balance and don't want to waste their money paying interest when they could be clearing the balance. However, it is not a free transfer; you will be charged on average 2% or 3% of the outstanding balance when you transfer to the new card. Banks generally only offer these cards to customers who have another one of their money products, such as a current account.

Beware: often these cards offer the first three months purchases at 0% interest, but these are often the last items to be paid off. If you have not cleared the whole balance by the end of the first three months, then you will begin to be charged interest on your purchases, *and* if you miss a payment or breach your credit limit you can lose your 0% interest period completely.

brilliant tip

Say you have a credit card with an uncleared balance and you have a good payment history. Applying for a 0% balance transfer credit card can work for you if you follow this rule: once you have received the card, transfer the balance and cut up the card. *Never use it.* Set in place a standing order to pay a regular amount every month, clearing the balance by the time the 0% balance transfer period ends. Job done!

Low-interest balance transfer credit card

Instead of a restricted period of 0% interest, this card offers a low interest rate for the life of the balance transferred. You will need to have a good payment history to receive one of these cards and generally need to be an existing customer of the card issuer.

Store card

This is a credit card that can only be used in one store or group of stores. The annual interest rates for these cards are high: quite often between 25% and 30%. This is because these cards are designed to make a profit from your purchases. The benefit for you may be that you get a discount off the price of your purchase. If you pay the balance off straight away, then all is well. If you don't, then you are charged more in interest than you have saved on your purchase.

brilliant example

Peter's wife, Helen, decided they needed new furniture for the family room. She chose the furniture at her local department store and went to order and pay. The store girl told her that if she applied for a store card she would get 10% off everything on her list. Helen had planned to spend ▶

£1,500 so that meant she would save £150. She signed the form. Instead of using her normal credit card, she used the store card, thinking they were the same. She did not read all the terms and conditions – who does? – since the print was too small without her glasses. When the statement arrived the interest rate was actually double the rate she would pay on her normal card, meaning that if she did not pay the balance off quickly her discount would actually cost her more in the long run. She used her normal credit card to pay the full balance on the store card then cancelled it – allowing her to have the discount without paying the high price.

never sign anything that you don't fully understand

Never sign anything that you don't fully understand. If I said 'Would you please sign a contract saying I can charge you any amount of money in the future – I will tell you later how much it is and when I will take it' would you sign it? That is what you are doing when you sign an agreement without reading it or having it explained.

Cash-back credit card

Every time you purchase something with this card you get an amount credited to your account equal to a set percentage of the amount spent. Effectively the credit card company gives you a discount on your purchases. However, the interest rate on the unpaid balance for these cards is generally higher than average.

brilliant example

Rob decided to buy a TV ready for when he and Andrew moved into their flat. His parents agreed to pay for it as a moving/congratulations-on-getting-your-degree present. Rob's parents are brilliant at personal finances, so they use a credit card that gives them cash back because they know they will always pay the balance in full when the statement arrives. Their card gives them 2% back on every purchase. The TV cost £700.00 and so they were given £14.00 back on their credit card.

Travel rewards credit card

This card will give you travel miles and discounts based on every £1 you spend. Some cards will require you to pay an annual fee but also offer extra features, such as free travel-related insurances. To apply for these cards you will need at least a good credit report.

Prepaid card

This is the opposite to a credit card. It requires no credit checks and no bank account. You either pay a monthly fee to have the card or a fee based on a percentage of your spending. You pay money into the card account in advance of spending it and then use the card just like a credit card or cash card. You can use it instead of a bank account and have your income paid directly into the card account.

Credit cards advertised for people with poor credit

These cards have extortionate interest rates. One card I reviewed had an annual interest rate of 39.9%. If you had on average a balance of £100 outstanding for a year then you would pay £39.90 in interest. *Avoid these cards.* Go for a prepaid card instead.

Making decisions about debts

Now that we have reviewed the different types of credit cards and store cards available, your task is to look at the cards you currently have with an outstanding balance. Ask yourself: 'Do they suit my purpose? Am I using them correctly or are they costing me more than I need to pay?'

You also need to review any other debts you may have.

Do you have a bank loan or overdraft?

- A *bank loan* is usually an unsecured loan. This means that, unlike a mortgage, there is no specific item that you own that the lender can repossess if you fail to repay the money borrowed.

- An *overdraft* facility is an agreement that you can spend more than you have in your bank account up to a specific amount.

Both bank loans and overdrafts have fees and interest charges with penalties for breaking the agreement designed to give the lender their reward. The bank or building society can withdraw an overdraft facility at any time so long as it gives the agreed notice. A loan can generally only be withdrawn if you break those rules of the agreement that give the lender the right to cancel.

So when do you use an overdraft facility rather than a loan? The simple answer is, when you need an extra amount of money that you have not already saved for a short period of time, say one or two months, and can then bring your account back to normal.

The situation

You have a bank loan, hire purchase agreement, student loan or some other form of finance debt.

Considerations

The first question that needs to be answered is, 'Can I pay the debt off faster than I am at the moment without making unacceptable changes to my life?' The key word is *unacceptable* not uncomfortable. If the answer is yes, then find out how that will reduce the cost of your debt and when could the debt be completely paid off. Remember the two rules of paying off loans faster: get the lowest interest rate and increase your monthly payments where you can.

Next, think about the fact that you have managed to find these payments every month to pay for these debts. When you no longer have to pay towards the debt, what can you do with the same – now extra – money to organise your life the way you want it to be? Add this to your wish list and, if this is an action you wish to take, now is the time to add it to your Action list (Table 1.1) at the front of the book.

Do you have unpaid tax?

If you are behind with your tax payments then again you will have broken an agreement. The agreement is with Her Majesty's Government. The one that says you will abide by the law of the land. In any scheme of clearing your debts, this debt should go to the top. Her Majesty's Revenue and Customs (HMRC) have the most power to recover money owed to them. But I don't want to scare you: all you need to do is talk to the tax office and explain your situation. Offer a payment plan that you can absolutely keep to. Generally, so long as you are being fair and honest, then the agreement will be accepted. It costs a lot of money to take you to court and send the bailiffs, so if you are willing to pay then most officials take the sensible option and let you.

brilliant tip

If you find yourself unable to save for a regular tax bill then set up a standing order to a savings account so that the money is removed from your regular account every month. If you really cannot stop yourself from dipping into the savings account then set up a direct debit with HMRC so that you pay a regular amount every month, in advance, towards the bill.

brilliant recap

Debt costs you money, so remember these principles:

- The reward you get for having a debt must be worth more than the cost of the debt.
- Use long-term debt for long-life purchases.
- Use short-term debt for short-life purchases.
- Overpaying on loans and mortgages can significantly reduce the cost and the term of the loan.

And finally . . .

Knowing your credit score (see Chapter 5) and what you are worth is only useful if you actually want to do something with that knowledge. Go back to the discovery you made in Chapter 2. Based on your reward in the short-, medium- and longer-term, think about what you need to do to change your net worth and credit score.

Let's take our three case studies as an example.

brilliant examples

Peter's goal is to reduce his debt and work towards starting a family. His net worth is positive because his debt has been used to buy things that still have some worth and his property is worth more than his mortgage. Peter's credit score is not excellent but not bad. He has a large amount of credit available to him and he currently meets all his payments on time. Peter has decided to sell some of the things he has that are of value and use the money to reduce his debt. He does not think this will make a significant difference to his net worth but if he clears and cancels some of his credit agreements then that will have a positive impact on his credit score and free up the money he pays out each month in interest. The money can go instead towards preparing to have a family.

Suzanne's goal is to travel. This will probably mean that she will not focus much on her net worth for the moment. She does not have a great deal of debt. She will need credit cards to use on her travels and in particular cards that reward her in air miles. With this in mind, she will focus on making sure her credit report is clean and shows that she is reliable, so giving her the best chance of the cheapest deals and rewards.

Rob and **Andrew** have a negative net worth. This is because of their student loans and the fact that they have not accumulated much in the way of possessions. They also have a pretty empty credit report and therefore a low credit score. Moving into their own flat gives them the opportunity to open utility accounts and other credit accounts in their own name and address. They have decided to split responsibility for the bills. Each of them will take on a specific bill that will be paid by direct debit from their bank accounts. They have also agreed they will register to vote as soon as they move in.

CHAPTER 9

Planning for the life you want – Part 1

Financial advice

If I wanted to become a tramp, I would seek information and advice from the most successful tramp I could find. If I wanted to become a failure, I would seek advice from men who have never succeeded. If I wanted to succeed in all things, I would look around me for those who are succeeding, and do as they have done.

Joseph Marshall Wade

Now that you understand a little more about how the money products work and you have worked out a future reward, it is time to start thinking about how to put your financial plan together. You may be feeling a little apprehensive. The last chapter may well have increased your understanding of the financial world but it has not made you an expert. So where can you go for help?

Free advice is available. You can go to your local Citizens Advice Bureau if you need help with sorting through your debts. You can also talk to Consumer Direct if you need advice on dealing with consumer-related contracts. However, the big question is still:

Do I need a financial adviser?

- If you were planning to run a marathon, you would probably find someone who knew how to train for the event and take advice. You might even employ a personal trainer to help you achieve the fitness you need to complete the task.

- If you were going to make some changes to your life that affected your health, then you would consult your doctor or a health professional.
- If you were buying an expensive piece of equipment, you would talk to some kind of expert to make sure you were making the right choice.

So it makes sense that if you are making decisions about how you use your money in the future you should find an expert who can help you. Ultimately the answer is yes, at some point in your life you should use a financial adviser. But use them wisely.

What is a financial adviser?

A financial adviser, in terms of personal finance, can be a financial planner but will also be a money salesperson. Their product is money. The money they sell comes in all different packages and brands. As with all products you buy, there are features and benefits that are reflected in the price. Unlike other products, however, your financial health and the health of those you are financially associated with also affect the price you pay. The credit score of you and your associates will be taken into account. (For a reminder of how to improve your credit score, go back to Chapter 5.)

▶ brilliant example

A loan is one example of a money product. A Barclay loan is a branded money product. The product you buy is the right to rent their money until you give it back. The rent you pay is called interest. The money always belongs to Barclays and they can ask for it back if you stop paying the rent on time.

How to choose a financial adviser

Financial advisers come in all shapes and sizes. That is to say, they are not all the same and cannot sell you the same range of products or advice. You need to ask a few questions to make sure that you get the adviser that suits your need. Here are the key questions to ask.

What qualifications do you have and what are you qualified to advise on?

For the basic level of advice, the adviser must have one or both of the following, or an equivalent qualification recognised by the Financial Services Authority:

- **Certificate in Financial Planning (Cert FP).** This allows someone to provide financial advice.

- **Certificate in Mortgage Advice and Practice (CeMAP).** This allows the adviser to give advice on mortgage products.

For more specialised advice, look for the following qualifications:

- **Diploma in Financial Planning (DipPFS).** This adviser will have an understanding of a broad range of areas, including taxation (both business and personal), trusts, pensions and investments.

- **Advanced Diploma in Financial Planning (APFS).** This adviser will have developed specialist planning capabilities.

- **Chartered Financial Planner.** This adviser has had at least five years' relevant industry experience and at least three years' continuous professional development. They also follow the Chartered Insurance Institute code of ethics.

- **Certified Financial Planner (CFP).** As well as possessing the diploma qualification, this adviser will have at least three years' industry experience. They will have been assessed through the use of a case study to make sure they can apply their knowledge practically.

- **Associate of Chartered Insurance Institute (ACII).** This adviser, if they do not hold any other qualification, will really only have focused on general insurance and is likely to be employed by an insurance company.

- **BSc (Hons) in Financial Services and Associateship (BSc (Hons) ACIB).** This adviser will have a degree-level qualification awarded by the Institute of Financial Services.

You can double-check if an adviser has the right qualifications to help you by looking on the Financial Services Authority Register at www.fsa.gov.uk/register/home.do or by ringing their consumer helpline.

Are you independent or tied?

- A **tied financial adviser** offers advice and sells one company's financial products. They don't generally offer all-round financial planning advice.

- A **multi-tied financial adviser** offers advice and sells more than one company's financial products.

- An **independent financial adviser** (IFA) is completely independent from the companies whose products are available to be sold. This does not mean that the adviser has access to all products on the market. Ask the question to be sure.

What area of financial advice do you specialise in?

You first need to know what you want from an adviser, and then find an adviser who has experience in that area. If you want to know about pensions, then don't go to a mortgage adviser.

How long have you been working in this area?

You are looking for someone you can relate to and who can help you plan for the future.

---

brilliant example

Rob's parents, Karen and Michael, had a mortgage that was only 15% of the value of the home they were living in. They wanted to use the equity in their home to invest in rental property to create income for their future. They chose a local independent financial adviser, with the relevant qualifications, to advise on how to implement their plan. Because the adviser had represented clients in the area for over 10 years he had relationships with the local estate agents and understood the local property market.

When Karen and Michael had a property in mind they were able to take it to their adviser, who helped them with the right offer price and potential return on investment to expect from the rental property. He also made sure that the estate agents they were dealing with understood exactly what they should be offering the couple. Ultimately, the IFA protected Karen and Michael from making hasty and uninformed decisions that may have affected their future income.

How will you be paid?

Independent financial advisers must offer you a choice of paying a fee for their service or allowing them to take a commission on the product they sell you.

 example

Peter does not necessarily need to buy a money product. He needs advice to help take control of his finances and plan for the future. An independent fee-based financial adviser qualified at certified or chartered level would be an appropriate choice, making sure that he ends up with the right level of expertise.

How to prepare for your first IFA meeting

an adviser can only give advice based on the information in front of them

Like any meeting, you get the most from it if you are well prepared. Whichever way you choose to pay – commission or fee – you want to get the best advice. Remember, an adviser can only give advice based on the information in front of them, so if you forget to tell them something relevant you may end up with the wrong advice.

Before you provide any information to the financial adviser they will make sure they have explained the service they offer. This will include the fact that they are regulated by the Financial Services Authority and how their fees and commissions are charged. At this point, if you choose to engage them on a fee basis rather than commission, ask them what will happen to the commission earned on any money products you buy as a result of their advice (in this case the commission may be passed to you).

If you have worked through the previous chapters, you will have recorded your chosen rewards and priorities. Take these with you and explain their importance in your first meeting.

The adviser will want to understand your current financial

position. Your actual net worth and your actual income and expenses history, from Chapters 4 and 6, will provide a picture of your financial situation and give clues to potential areas for improvement.

As well as the above documents it will be useful if you bring any financial agreements you already have, such as:

- mortgages;
- loans;
- insurances;
- income protection cover;
- ISAs;
- endowments;
- stock options;
- savings plans.

During the meeting the financial adviser will ask you lots of questions. One should be about your attitude to risk. Remember Chapter 3, where you reviewed your money personality. Share how safe you need to feel, in money terms, with the adviser. It will help explain how much risk you are prepared to take with your money.

Following the meeting, the adviser should follow up, in writing, with a summary of the information shared and also document the advice, or agreed action points, from the meeting. If, at any stage, you do not understand the information being put before you then ask for an explanation in ever more lay terms. Remember, a financial adviser provides advice, not decisions. The decisions are yours and you can only make good decisions if you understand the advice you are given.

a financial adviser provides advice, not decisions

There is nothing wrong with taking time to make sure the right decision is taken. A financial adviser has built up knowledge of the financial world and its products over a long period of time. You, however, understand your own life and financial needs far better than any adviser. This puts you on an equal footing in knowledge terms. Don't feel intimidated because they have studied their subject: you are paying them to know their subject. Remember, you are the client and are paying for a service.

brilliant tip

Never feel that you should be in a hurry to make a decision just because the adviser is impatient and pushing for an answer. Ask the adviser why a fast decision is needed. If they say it is because there is a time limit on the offer, ask them to show you the details and explain how much it will cost if you do not decide in time. Make sure you understand the decision deadlines and available cooling-off period so that you can change your mind if you need to.

When you don't need a paid financial adviser

It will not be appropriate to spend money engaging a financial adviser if you are already in extreme trouble with debt. If you find yourself with people sending, or threatening to send, bailiffs to your door, then you need more specialist advice than this book can offer and in a manner that does not increase your debt.

brilliant tip

If you are being chased constantly for money and you see no way out, don't panic and don't ignore it. *Talk* to experts who can help you take action. Contact a not-for-profit organisation who will give you one-to-one advice. At the very least, a debt counselling organisation can get you 30 days of not being chased while they try to help you sort out a plan of action.

The following organisations are specifically set up to help you get through the tough decisions needed when your debt is out of control:

- National Debtline: www.nationaldebtline.co.uk
- Citizens Advice: www.adviceguide.org.uk (or a local office)
- Consumer Credit Counselling Service: www.cccs.co.uk
- Christians Against Poverty: www.capuk.org

These organisations will not charge for providing you with help. This means that any money you have available to pay off your debts can go straight to the people you owe money to.

If you use the internet or see adverts from organisations that offer debt-clearing advice and help, do not use them without first understanding how they get paid for the help they offer.

brilliant recap

Using an expert to help you make informed decisions is a smart move. Here is a summary of the points to remember.

- Go to not-for-profit organisations if your debt situation is out of control.
- When looking for a financial adviser, make sure they are suitably qualified for your needs by asking the following key questions:
  - What qualifications do you have and what are you qualified to advise on?
  - Are you independent or tied?
  - What area of financial advice do you specialise in?
  - How long have you been working in this area?
  - How will you be paid?
- Be well prepared for the first meeting. Make sure that you:
  - know what you want from your finances;
  - bring with you your net worth and income and expenses analysis;
  - bring with you any relevant existing financial documents.

▶

- Understand the fees involved.

- Listen to the advice but make your own decisions.

We will now move on to the second part of planning for the life you want, where you will put together your own plan with specific action points that you can start to implement immediately.

CHAPTER 10

Planning for the life you want – Part 2

Action plan

Luck is good planning, carefully executed.

Anonymous

In this chapter we will focus on putting together an immediate action plan: a to-do list. This specific plan is to work out the actions you need to take to work towards your goals and rewards. In the next chapter we will develop an ongoing approach to planning so that you will constantly be in control and ready to make changes and take decisions without having to take time out to assess your situation. In other words, we'll be building financial planning and control into your everyday life.

If you look back at your short-term and your medium-term rewards and goals, these should all fit into one or more of the following action categories:

1 Be in control and stop wasting money.

2 Reduce or clear debt.

3 Save or borrow efficiently for a specific event or purchase.

4 Plan for future income or retirement.

The first action underpins all the others. This is because it will release money to be used towards your goals.

Completing your plan

You may find that your goals involve action in more than one of the above categories. To make life easier and to stop you from making a list so long that it seems impossible to achieve, use Table 10.1 to list the most important action points in each category. One of the most important items in the table is the column marked 'By this date'. Give yourself a deadline and a small reward for completing the tasks by the date set. It will give you the motivation to keep going as you can feel you are getting somewhere.

Use the information recorded in tables from previous sections of the book as we work through each action category. They will help you decide on your own specific plan. The tables to use are:

- Table 1.1 on page 11 (action list)
- Tables 4.1, 4.2, 4.3 and 4.4 on pages 45, 47, 49 and 50 (income and expenses)
- Table 6.1 on page 87 (net worth).

The way to use the table is to start using it with your short-term goals. Put them in the column headed 'I/we will have achieved' . Put the goal in as many categories as it relates to. Don't put a completion date on it without first thinking about all the actions needed first. Then realistically think about how long it will take you to complete them. Putting an unrealistic deadline will only set you up to fail. Be realistic; put a date you really think is achievable.

Table 10.1 Action plan

Action category	By this date	I/we will have achieved	Through these actions
Be in control and stop wasting money			1 2 3 4
Reduce or clear debt			1 2 3 4
Save or borrow efficiently for a specific event or purchase			1 2 3 4
Plan for future income or retirement			1 2 3 4

Action category 1: Be in control and stop wasting money

No bailiffs at the door? – then read on.

At this point you need the completed tables from Chapter 4. These need to be fully complete with real numbers, not the ones you filled in on the bus, train or plane from memory.

The first step to being in control of your finances is to make sure that from now on you do not have late payment or interest fees, or that money going out exceeds the money coming in. Use Table 10.2 to help you identify wasted money or opportunities for releasing cash for use towards your goals. As we go through the next few pages, fill in Table 10.2 so that you can see how much money can be released.

Table 10.2 Potential cash

	Month 1	Month 2	Month 3
A: Money left over or overspent (from row E in Table 4.4)			
B: Less unnecessary spend			
C: Less extravagant spend			
D: Money left over or overspent			

Identify the unnecessary

Unnecessary spending is money going out that gives you no benefit, remember, this may be related to your money personality. On your no-choice spending list (Table 4.2 on page 47) check if you have any of the following charges:

Parking fines

You will incur parking fines if you often underestimate how long you will be. Make a note to yourself always to pay for half an hour more than you need. Spending an extra 50p is better than a £12 fine you either can't afford or you could spend on something else. Make a note of how much you could have saved.

Late payment credit card charges

There is no excuse for these charges. You know you have to pay every month, yet you leave it to the last minute to pay the balance and miss the deadline. Set up a direct debit with your credit card company to pay the minimum amount. This will always avoid the late payment charges. You can always top up your minimum payment to clear the balance in full if you want.

Unauthorised overdraft fees and returned unpaid items fee

Look at your money coming in and money going out and make sure that there is enough time between your salary payments and your outgoing direct debits for the money to be available. The only way to fix this permanently is to work to a budget. The next chapter will show you how to do this as part of your monthly routine.

brilliant tip

If your personality means that no matter how important something is you will probably forget to do it on time, then get someone else to do it. For example, get the company you need to pay to collect their payment by direct debit.

Insurances

I am not suggesting here that insurance is an unnecessary item. But sometimes we find ourselves insured twice for the same thing. We could also be over-insured. Look at your insurance policies to check that you are not paying for something you do not need. If you think you are, then make a phone call to your insurance provider to see if your premiums would be reduced if you reduce the value of your cover.

Have you been with the same insurance provider while just accepting the renewal premiums? Take time out to check if they are competitive. If your premium is too high compared to the competition, tell your provider you are planning to switch. They may match the competitive offer and reduce your premiums.

All other contracts with service providers

Use this same approach to ask for better deals with your mobile phone provider and other utilities. If you don't ask, you don't get. The worst you can get is 'No, we can't change the price'. In this case you may want to take your business elsewhere as soon as your contract allows.

When you have found all the items you think fall into the unnecessary spend category, add up the cost of all the items and put them into row B of Table 10.2.

Identify the extravagant

I would expect that most of your extravagant items are those that you identified in Table 4.3. There are probably items on this list that you pay for but don't give you value for money. Use the following questions as a prompt for what to include on the list:

- Do you have a gym or club subscription that you hardly use and would be cheaper if you switched to pay-as-you-go?

- Do you have subscriptions to online services that you do not use?

- Are there magazines or papers you buy or have delivered that are still in the wrapper?

- Do you have extra TV stations on satellite or cable TV that you never watch or could do without?

- Have you developed a habit of going out for a meal or getting a takeaway just because you can't be bothered to cook?

- Do you buy lunch, coffee or snacks while out or at work that you could bring from home?

Include anything on the list that you might give up for a while or could do with less frequently if there was a very good reason. Now add the total of your extravagant list together for each month and put it in row C of Table 10.2.

What it all means

Let's see how much of a difference that makes to your finances. Take the totals for Month 1 row B and row C away from row A and put your answer in row D. Do the same for Months 2 and 3. How does it look now?

Overspend has gone down but not gone away
If this is the result, then go back and check your choice money out list in Table 4.3 on page 49 again and see if there are any other items you could lose for a short period of time to balance your finances. If you can't find anything, then you may find you need to sell some possessions or seek one-to-one debt advice.

Overspend has turned into money left over
Good news! Now you just have to cancel the subscriptions and find a way not to do the things you have identified as too extravagant. Add your action points for this category to your action plan using Table 10.1 on page 153.

Finally, take the action points from Chapters 7 and 8 that you made a note of in your ongoing action list (Table 1.1). When you looked at the money products you currently use, are there any smart changes to be made? For instance, do you have funds sitting in a low-interest account and so are you wasting money through not earning the best interest? Do you need to cancel your overdraft facility to stop you overspending?

Action category 2: Reduce or clear debt

Let's return to Table 10.1. Now we need to refer back to the list of debts in Table 6.1: your net worth (page 87). This way we can generate a list of the debts you want to clear. Most people who have several balances on different cards or loans try to pay a bit off all of them each month and hope that over time they can clear all the balances completely.

> aim to get the most from the money you have

That may work, but it will not be the most efficient way of doing it. Remember, the aim is to get the most from the money you have.

Credit and store card debt

If you have not cleared your debt on credit or store cards, then every month you will be charged an amount of interest. If you only have a fixed amount of money available to put towards your debts then you first pay the interest charge and then whatever is left over reduces the amount of debt you have outstanding. To clear your debts, you need to get rid of the ones that charge the most interest first.

Let's look at an example.

 **example**

Suzanne has two store cards:

● Card A charges 2% interest each month and she has a balance of £200.

● Card B charges 0.5% interest each month and also has a balance of £200.

She has £50 available to pay towards her debt and splits it evenly between both cards (i.e. she pays £25 towards each card each month).

The minimum payment required is £5 per month, or the interest if that is higher.

Table 10.3 Payment plan

	Card A			Card B		
	Balance	2% Interest	Payment	Balance	0.5% Interest	Payment
Month 1	£200.00	£4.00	−£25.00	£200.00	£1.00	−£25.00
Month 2	£179.00	£3.58	−£25.00	£176.00	£0.88	−£25.00
Month 3	£157.58	£3.15	−£25.00	£151.88	£0.76	−£25.00
Month 4	£135.73	£2.71	−£25.00	£127.64	£0.64	−£25.00
Month 5	£113.45	£2.27	−£25.00	£103.28	£0.52	−£25.00
Month 6	£90.72	£1.81	−£25.00	£78.79	£0.39	−£25.00
Month 7	£67.53	£1.35	−£25.00	£54.19	£0.27	−£25.00
Month 8	£43.88	£0.88	−£25.00	£29.46	£0.15	−£25.00
Month 9	£19.76	£0.40	−£20.15	£4.61	£0.02	−£4.63
TOTAL		£20.15	−£220.15		£4.63	−£204.63

As Table 10.3 shows, this plan will cost Suzanne £24.78 in interest and it takes nine months to pay off both cards.

The more efficient way would be to pay the minimum amount on the cheapest card and use the rest of her £50 to pay the more expensive card. Table 10.4 shows how this works.

Table 10.4 Revised payment plan

	Card A			Card B		
	Balance	2% Interest	Payment	Balance	0.5% Interest	Payment
Month 1	£200.00	£4.00	−£45.00	£200.00	£1.00	−£5.00
Month 2	£159.00	£3.18	−£45.00	£196.00	£0.98	−£5.00
Month 3	£117.18	£2.34	−£45.00	£191.98	£0.96	−£5.00
Month 4	£74.52	£1.49	−£45.00	£187.94	£0.94	−£5.00
Month 5	£31.01	£0.62	−£31.63	£183.88	£0.92	−£18.37
Month 6	£0.00	£0.00	£0.00	£166.43	£0.83	−£50.00
Month 7	£0.00	£0.00	£0.00	£117.27	£0.59	−£50.00
Month 8	£0.00	£0.00	£0.00	£67.85	£0.34	−£50.00
Month 9	£0.00	£0.00	£0.00	£18.19	£0.09	−£18.28
TOTAL		£11.63	−£211.63		£6.65	−£206.65

Following the more efficient payment method, Suzanne will pay £6.50 less in interest (a total of £18.28, rather than £24.78). She will also have a sense of achievement as one card will be completely paid off in five months.

Now, £6.50 is not a large amount of money, but it does stay in Suzanne's pocket rather than the pocket of the credit card company. This must be a good thing. The real advantage comes when the debt is larger or the payments smaller.

Here is another example from our case studies.

brilliant example

Peter has two store cards, both with £2,000 outstanding. He has the same interest rates per month, just like Suzanne, and can put £200 each month towards paying off the debt.

If Peter pays £100 each month towards each debt, this would happen.

● Card A would be paid off in 26 months.

● Card B would be paid off in 22 months.

● It will cost him £705.85 in interest.

If instead Peter paid only the minimum amount towards the cheaper card and the rest to the more expensive card until it was paid off, then this would happen:

● Card A would be paid off in 12 months.

● Card B would be paid off in 23 months.

● It would cost him £444.48 in interest.

The principle of paying off the card with more interest first is more effective the higher the debt. In our example Peter would be store-card debt-free three months earlier, having completely cleared one of the cards within 12 months. He would also save himself £261.37 in interest. Now that would be worth doing!

How to organise your card debt payment efficiently

Take the debts you have and organise them in order of how expensive they are in terms of interest payments. Generally, the most expensive debt is the short-term credit or store card debt. Before we embark on clearing the debts, cut up the credit and store cards whose debt you are trying to clear. Don't use them: adding to your debt will reduce the impact of your payments.

Now follow these steps:

1 If your credit score is good, you could obtain a 0% balance transfer card and transfer debt, starting with the most expensive first.

2 If you cannot get a 0% balance transfer card, then you could see if you are able to get a cheaper percentage interest card than the ones you have and use it to pay off the most expensive debt first.

3 If steps 1 and 2 are unavailable to you, then check if your cheaper cards have any credit limit available. Use these cards to pay off the more expensive debt.

4 If you have not done so already, set up direct debits to pay the minimum due on all debt so that you do not incur any extra fees for late payments.

5 Work out the maximum you can pay towards your debt each month. Top up your payment to the most expensive debt after paying the minimum payments. For example, if you have £200 available and your total minimum payments this month add up to £35, then pay an extra £165 (the money you have left) towards the most expensive debt.

6 When the most expensive debt is paid off, move to the next most expensive debt using the same process, and always keeping your total debt payment at the same level or more.

brilliant tip

If your debt situation means that you are considering bankruptcy or an individual voluntary arrangement, then talk to the credit card company and make them a payment offer to clear the debt. Ask them to freeze the interest and to accept a regular amount each month until the debt is cleared. If they think this is the best way to recover their money, they may agree. The free not-for-profit advice centres mentioned in the last chapter will help negotiate.

Longer-term debt issues

There is another form of debt relating to your mortgage that may be causing you a problem.

The situation

You have an endowment policy and are depending on this policy to repay your mortgage. The last forecast received from the provider of the endowment policy shows that it will not be enough to pay the full mortgage amount that will be due. You have already looked into claiming compensation and the claim has been dealt with. You still have a shortfall between the mortgage amount due and the money that will available from the policy.

Possible actions

In this situation you will benefit from talking to a financial adviser who specialises in mortgages so that you can gather information on the specific options available to you (see Chapter 9 for more information about choosing a financial adviser). The specific answer to your situation will depend on understanding *your* specific financial situation, the size of the shortfall and how much time you have left before you have to pay back the money. There are a number of things you can think about (but remember that being accepted for new loans will depend on your credit score and the value of your home versus the loan being applied for):

● Convert the part of your mortgage that constitutes the shortfall to a repayment mortgage so that the interest-only mortgage is reduced and you are able to pay it in full when the time comes. This is likely to increase your monthly outgoings.

● Sell or cash in your endowment policy and remortgage, possibly to a repayment mortgage, using the money received from the endowment policy to reduce the amount you need to borrow as part of your remortgage. This may or may not increase your monthly outgoings.

● Find another savings plan to accumulate the funds to plug the gap. This will also increase your monthly outgoings.

● Sell something of value to raise the funds to plug the gap. You will need to be sure that the valuation remains high enough for this strategy to work.

● Do nothing now and rely on selling the property, downsizing and using the profit made to pay the mortgage shortfall. This is a more risky option.

The point here is that whatever option you choose it is important to have a plan: one that fits your circumstances and your goals.

Before we move to the next category, add your action points to Table 10.1.

Action category 3: Save or borrow efficiently for a specific event or purchase

As we have demonstrated in previous chapters, saving for an event or large purchase in the future is cheaper if you save in advance and use the power of compounding to generate the lump sum you need.

But what if you can buy the item now, with a 0% interest finance arrangement?

Situation 1

You want to buy a flat-screen TV costing £1,000. You have the option of 0% finance on the purchase spreading your payments over 24 months or paying a lump sum in 24 months. But if you do not clear the balance by the end of the 24th month then the full interest of 12% will be charged from the day of purchase.

Possible action

Set up a savings plan that will guarantee the required amount in 23 months and then transfer the lump-sum savings to pay for your purchase. You will pay into the plan less than £1,000 because you will earn interest on your savings, and you will be guaranteed to pay the balance off before the due date.

Alternatively you may be tempted by the same purchase in the sales, with a 10% discount:

Situation 2

The TV on sale costs £1,000. It is offered at 10% discount and so you pay £900.

Possible action

If you do not have the cash to pay right now, then you can use a 0% purchase credit card or relatively cheap interest rate credit card to buy the TV. However, before you buy, call the credit card company. Ask how much interest you will pay on a £900 purchase based on the monthly payments you are definitely able to make. If the interest is less than £100, then you still have a bargain. So you can still have a bargain in the sales without saving first if you borrow and pay back wisely.

Your action points here should be about how you are going to organise your finances to pay for an item or event you are planning for.

Action category 4: Plan for future income or retirement

In this category you will need to record any action points noted in relation to your assets and potential retirement or pension income. We noted earlier in Chapter 6 (the basics of contributing to a pension) that this is a complicated area. If you do not have any pension arrangements, then possibly your first two action points will be:

- Decide what you need as income.
- Find a suitable financial adviser to explain what your options are.

Using your plan

This is where you begin to take charge of your finances. You should by now have a list of practical tasks to be completed by a specific date that will make a difference to your finances. Don't forget to have a small reward when you complete a significant task to help keep you motivated.

Ideally, you should not move on to the next part of the planning process until this one is complete. Good luck with the tasks.

⤢ brilliant recap

- Your plan should focus on obtaining your short- and medium-term rewards.

- Use the following action categories to help define your action plan:
  - be in control and stop wasting money;
  - reduce or clear debt;
  - save or borrow efficiently for a specific event or purchase;
  - plan for future income or retirement.

- To stay in control, simplify your finances and automate your payments:
  - identify the unnecessary and take action to remove it;
  - identify the extravagant and decide whether you need or want to continue spending the money.

- Find the most efficient way to reduce your debts:
  - pay the most expensive debt off first;
  - pay the minimum amount on other debts so that you do not break your agreements;
  - take advice from not-for-profit organisations that support people in debt.

- When considering an expensive purchase, compare the cost of saving before spending with borrowing and paying back after the purchase; if possible, take the cheapest option. (Remember to factor in your ability to be disciplined in saving and repayment plans.)

- When planning your retirement, work out how much income you need and then find out from an expert how much you need in a lump sum to create that income in the future.

CHAPTER 11

Making brilliant personal finances a lifelong habit

Everything is in the mind. That's where it all starts. Knowing what you want is the first step toward getting it.

Mae West, American film actress

So far the exercises and information in this book have focused on increasing your understanding of the money system and your own finances. We started the journey with finding out what was most important to you in terms of managing your money, and in the last chapter you put together your action list. This chapter is about how you build good personal finance management into your daily life. There is no getting away from it, developing good habits takes time and effort. But I am sure you will agree that if it gets you the reward you want, then it is worth putting the effort in.

We are now going to cover:

- five principles to live by;
- how to make straightforward financial decisions;
- how to find the time to put and keep your finances in order;
- monthly planning and budgeting;
- everyday habits that will help;
- how to keep track of where you are.

Five principles to live by

Principle 1: Know your goal and use it to make decisions

We've talked about this a lot, and if you're committed to sorting out your finances – and if you've used the book sensibly – then we don't need to say more about this.

Principle 2: Be bothered

This covers a multitude of things.

- Be bothered to cook rather than order an unplanned takeaway or go out to eat.
- Be bothered to look for bargains or research the price of a large purchase.
- Be bothered to compare quotes and negotiate at renewal time.
- Be bothered to get group discounts.
- Be bothered to wait and save for something you don't need right now.
- Be bothered to develop good financial habits.
- Be bothered to take time to plan.

The list can go on and on. I am sure you have got the point. By being bothered you will naturally stop wasting money and be on top of your financial situation.

Principle 3: File and organise your paper

Now I quite understand if this is a difficult one for you. I am not a naturally organised person. Without the principle of being bothered I would quite happily have all my paper in one big pile in the corner of the room. My thought process goes along the lines of 'If it is all in one place, then I will know where to look if I ever need it'. The problem with that approach is that I would waste so much of my life looking through the same bits of paper over and over.

I suggest that you get yourself a couple of ring binders. If life is complicated, have one for the house and one for personal items; or have more files, if you really are overloaded with paper. Add a set of cardboard multicoloured dividers with a tab to each file. At the front of the house file and the personal file add a blank sheet of paper. This is where you can write down all the contact details of the people you may have to talk to if there is a problem. As you get a new bill, insurance statement or bank statement, then hole-punch it and put it in the file. Fill the sections of the files from front to back, writing something on each tab to let you know what you will find there. Unless there is a good reason to keep them, destroy old insurance documents or last year's gas bills as the new ones are filed. Eventually you will have one place with all the latest information you need to manage your finances.

 **example**

Table 11.1 shows an extract from the front page of Peter's household file.

Table 11.1 Household details

Name of organisation	What they do	How they are paid	Address	Telephone/e-mail
TalkTalk	Broadband and phone supplier	Direct debit: 1st		
Inchcape Finance	Car finance	Direct debit: 3rd		
Direct Line	House and contents cover	Monthly direct debit: 10th		
British Gas	Gas and electric	Cheque: quarterly		

Principle 4: Do not ignore bills

Always open the brown envelopes, and if you cannot pay on time then let people know. Human beings don't like to be ignored and if the human beings are ignored then the automated computer systems just spit out standard letters and assume you will never pay. Many people end up with court judgments for not paying bills just because they did not pick up the phone and explain.

Principle 5: Use a calendar to plan

The reason for having a calendar will become clear later in the chapter, but the basic idea is that to be in control you need to plan ahead and know what is coming your way. Most people use a calendar or diary of some sort. If they don't, then they have access to one, either on their computer or their phone. Ideally, a calendar or diary should be part of your everyday life. If you are a family with relatively young children, then you probably have a calendar on the wall or fridge in the living area. If you work in an office, then you will have one on your PC. If you are on the move, then the one on your phone will work fine. The main point is to keep things simple and conveniently part of your everyday activity.

> to be in control you need to plan ahead

How to make straightforward financial decisions

Spending decisions

1   Take a piece of paper and write your life goal(s) at the top.

2   Then write down the decision you need to make.

3   Ask the question 'Will spending the money take me towards my goal(s)?'

   ● A 'No' answer and you should really stop there.

- A 'Yes' answer then on to the next step.

4 Use Table 11.2 to compare your options. Write in an option on each line.

5 Choose the cheapest option that you can afford, based on when you need the item.

Table 11.2 Spending options

What are you buying?	How will you plan to pay for it (i.e. savings, credit card, HP etc.)?	When will you get the item?	What is the set-up cost?	What will it cost per month?	What will be the total cost over the time to pay?

brilliant example

Peter has a credit card that he uses for larger purchases. His credit score is not great, so he is not eligible for the best 0% interest credit card. The credit card he has shows an annual interest rate of 16.6%. On the internet he sees a flat-screen TV that normally retails for £1,300 reduced to £1,100. All his friends have a large flat-screen TV and he feels the pressure to keep up with everyone else. As the offer expires the same week, he has enough credit limit on his credit card, so he places the order. He thinks that if he pays a bit off each month he would have saved himself £200.

In fact Peter only really manages to pay the minimum balance each month. At this rate it will take him 12 years to pay for the TV and cost him an extra £636. Not such a bargain at all.

Peter's downfall is not that he does not understand the cost of credit cards but that he has not kept in mind his life goal and reward. When Peter looked at what he wanted from his life in one year, he said 'I want less debt and to plan to start a family'. Yet by adding another purchase to his credit card he has increased his debt and moved further away from his goal.

Investing or saving decisions

The same principle can be used for investments.

1   Take a piece of paper and write your life goal(s) at the top.

2   Then write down the decision you need to make.

3   Ask the question 'Will investing the money take me towards or away from my goal(s)?'

    ● A 'No' answer and you should really stop there.

    ● A 'Yes' answer, then on to the next step.

4   Use Table 11.3 to compare what you get with what you invest. Write in an option on each line.

5   Choose the option that gives you the best return with the monthly investment you can afford, in light of your goals and other commitments.

Table 11.3 Investment options

What is the investment?	What are you guaranteed to get?	How much will you pay in total?	What is the monthly investment?	When will your investment mature?

Remember Tables 11.2 and 11.3 are just templates to help put the information in order. You may need to consider more information, provided by your financial adviser.

How to find the time to put and keep your finances in order

The question is, how much time do you need? If you have a long list of urgent actions, you may need to look at your weekly activities and put some things on hold. Could you give up watching a couple of TV programmes? Or use your lunch hour at work instead of going out to lunch? Just think about how you spend your time. Most people can rearrange their lives in the short term to begin the process of ordering their finances.

In the long run, you don't need to spend a great deal of time on keeping your finances under control. Just use the 'keep it simple' rule. If you make your financial life as simple and straightforward as possible, then life will be less stressful and it won't take as long to plan and make decisions.

brilliant tips

- Pay all your bills by direct debit.
- Reduce the number of credit cards you carry to the three most useful ones.
- Automate payments to savings plans or investments by setting up standing orders or direct debits.
- If you do not use it already, set up online banking so that you can see your bank statement and balances whenever you want.
- Be really focused on what you want from your money.
- Keep a list of issues to be dealt with, but deal with them one at a time in order of importance.
- Set pocket money limits for everyone in the household – including you. It doesn't have to be a small amount but to be in control it should be fixed.

If you use all these tips then there will be a whole chunk of financial activity that no longer requires thinking about, leaving you time to focus on the future.

Monthly planning and budgeting

How to be in control for the rest of your life!

So here we are at the point where changing your habits for life begins. No matter how you look at it, to be in control you need to develop a regular planning and reviewing habit. The words *budget, budget* and *budget* come to mind. Followed by *review, review* and *review*.

But don't worry: as with all the tasks you face, you can use a handy template (Tables 11.4, 11.5 and 11.6) to get started. If you are happy to use a computer and spreadsheets, then these tables are available to download from: www.brilliantpersonalfinances.co.uk

Remember also Principle 5 at the beginning of this chapter: use a calendar. This is where the calendar becomes a useful tool. Think about how you use your calendar right now. You probably don't even think about the information you record – you just do it:

- If you are a family with small children, you may be used to using a calendar to keep track of activities, birthday parties and babysitting.

- If you work in a job that means you travel frequently, your calendar or diary may be full of flight details or meeting times and may be electronic and portable.

- A young person with few commitments will keep social-related dates and times, possibly again in a portable format.

- An older person may use a calendar as a reminder for birthdays and special occasions.

The key to making your monthly planning and budgeting less cumbersome is to build them into your daily routine.

 **example**

Suzanne uses her electronic calendar to keep track of when she is meant to meet up with her various groups of friends. She prints the calendar in month format and folds it in half to carry in her handbag. Each day while travelling to work on the train, she makes a note of her expected expenses for the next month. They are then ready to be transferred to her forecast on the third Thursday of the month, the evening she has set aside for completing her forecast and having a quiet night in.

Putting together your monthly plan

The next section will explain how to put a monthly plan of your financial commitments together. Why should you do this? The main reasons are to give you the opportunity to make sure you do not waste your money, and to give you the basis to make future decisions because you will know how much money is available; in short, to help you reach your goals.

So do you need to set aside a huge amount of time to plan? The answer is no, not if you use your equivalent of a calendar to record information over time. The only concentrated time you need to set aside is about two hours a month to fill in the template and review your situation.

What information do you need to record?

The information needed for the monthly forecast is the same information you used to put together your income and expenses Tables in Chapter 4. The only difference is that instead of looking back at what you have earned and spent, you are looking forward and predicting your income and spending.

Before you even think about completing the cash flow plan (Tables 11.4, 11.5, 11.6 and 11.7), get used to adding this information to your calendar as you think of it (see Figure 11.1). If you have never done this before, you may want to start with the next three months first, and then move on to six and then finally 12 months. When you have the template completed and you are using it to review and plan, the main task each month will be to discard the month just gone and add another month of forecast in the future. This way, you will always be planning ahead but only one month at a time.

March 2010 – House Calendar					
Monday	Tuesday	Wednesday	Thursday	Friday	Sat/Sun
1 March	2	3	4	5	6
School pocket money £9		House ins. £249		Joe's birthday £50	7
8	9	10	11	12	13
School pocket money £9	Car loan direct debit £112				14
15	16	17	18	19	20
School pocket money £9					Children's party Joe £10 21
22	23	24	25	26	27
School pocket money £9					28
29	30	31			
School pocket money £9	Car tax £215				

Figure 11.1 Sample calendar of expenses

The following categories will help jog your memory until it becomes second nature:

- **Bill payments**: Add the direct debit payments and what they are for on the day they are due out. Do the same for any other bills not paid by direct debit. If you do not know exactly what the amount will be, then put your best guess.

- **People events**: You may have these on the calendar already (birthdays, anniversaries, children's activities, etc.). You need to put a cost against these if you plan to spend money because of the event. Include all your social going-out activities.

- **Maintenance items**: No, this is not about having your hair done! This is the category that includes getting the car serviced, or the boiler serviced, or having the windows cleaned. Again, put the item and your expected spend on the relevant date.

- **Shopping events**: Don't ignore the need to spend on new clothes or personal grooming. You may not get the actual day right, but if you put it on the calendar in the right month then it will end up in your forecast.

- **Holiday events**: Put short and long breaks in on the days you think you will spend the money rather than when you take the holiday. Don't forget the spending money too.

- **School and community events**: These include any organised event or community activity that you may be involved with that means spending money. Add the event and your expected spend.

- **Forgotten events**: Every three months put an amount on the calendar for unexpected costs. Think back to the last time you were caught out with an unexpected bill and use that as a guide to how much you should put in.

- **Household shopping**: This may be easy or difficult, depending on whether you do a weekly shop or just buy a bit each day. Either way, include an estimate of how much you spend and include that amount as frequently as you need to reflect reality.

There will still be items that have not been included in the above list. Add everything you spend to your chosen calendar. If you wish, you can also add the income expected to the calendar; however, predicting your income is usually less complicated, so you may choose to put this information straight into the template rather than put it on a calendar or diary.

Your cash flow plan

The cash flow plan does not actually list your expenses: the first column in Tables 11.5 and 11.6 is for you to put the items relevant to you in the way that makes most sense. Just as in Chapter 4, the spending is split between those expenses that are currently fixed or are paid by direct debit and those expenses that you have a choice about. There are then two more sections (in Table 11.7) where you can add an amount for the unexpected, and also any extra payments you may make towards credit card or loan debt.

The second column is the first month of your forecast. Next to Month 1, write the name of the month, such as May 2011. Complete the forecast column for each month, adding up and recording the subtotal for each section. When you get to the end, there is a line where you can work out whether you are overspending or underspending.

If you are going to use a paper version of the template, then use a pencil rather than pen. This way, if you find you are overspending and want to reduce the amount you plan to spend on particular items, you can do this and recalculate your totals without having to cross out numbers.

Every time a month is finished, compare how much you actually spent with the plan. The easiest way to record this is to use your calendar again to record your cash spending against the planned amount, and consult your bank statements and credit card statements for everything else. You will then see where you got it wrong, forgot something and need to change your future plan.

That's the guidance over: now it is up to you!

Table 11.4 Cash flow plan: income

Income	Month 1			Month 2			Month 3		
	Forecast	Actual	Difference	Forecast	Actual	Difference	Forecast	Actual	Difference
Salary									
Freelance income									
Benefits									
Pension									
Maintenance									
Child support									
Investment income									
Rental income									
F: Total income									

Table 11.5 Cash flow plan: expenses – fixed or no choice

Expenses: Fixed or no choice	Month 1			Month 2			Month 3		
	Forecast	Actual	Difference	Forecast	Actual	Difference	Forecast	Actual	Difference
A: subtotal fixed expenses									

Table 11.6 Cash flow plan: expenses – discretionary or your choice

Expenses: discretionary or your choice	Month 1			Month 2			Month 3		
	Forecast	Actual	Difference	Forecast	Actual	Difference	Forecast	Actual	Difference
B: subtotal discretionary expenses									

Table 11.7 Cash flow plan: expenses – unplanned and debts

Expenses: unplanned	Month 1			Month 2			Month 3		
	Forecast	Actual	Difference	Forecast	Actual	Difference	Forecast	Actual	Difference
C: Subtotal unplanned									
Additional debt payments									
D: Subtotal debt payments									
E: Total expenses (A + B + C + D = E)									
Over/underspend F minus E									

Everyday habits that will help

We all need a few tips on making things easier for ourselves. If you want to keep control without great effort, here are a few things to consider.

- Use a fridge list – one of those magnetic note pads. When you begin to run low of a household item then add it to the list. This will mean that next time you go shopping you will have a ready-made list, saving you time and reducing your potential to buy what you don't actually need.

- Put loyalty vouchers and discount vouchers straight in the bag, purse or wallet that you will have with you when you shop – preferably near the payment card you will use, ready to hand over at the till. Don't put them on the pin board or fridge, or worse still in a drawer: they will never get used.

- If you manage your life by using a timetable or diary, make an appointment with yourself to make your lists or look at your finances. Make it as important to keep the date as all your other commitments.

- If you don't know how you spend so much each day on sundry items, give yourself a limited amount of pocket money and leave your debit or credit card at home. Having a limited amount to spend on lunch etc. will make you look at the price.

- When it comes to throwing something away that is not broken, ask yourself 'Would this be useful to someone else?' If the answer is yes, then sell it in the local paper or on the internet. Add the contact number or website address to the list at the front of your household file for easy reference.

- Get other people to remind you. For regular jobs like servicing the car, use a garage or mobile service that will keep a record of when your next service is likely to be due and tell them to call you and book it in. This will mean less clutter in your mind.

These are a few hints to get you started. I am sure if you start talking to your friends and family about how they control their finances, they will have some more useful tips for you.

How to keep track of where you are

It is all very well having a monthly forecast and organising your paper, but when life is busy during the month we all need a few triggers that say when things might not be going according to plan.

At the end of the month, when you compare your income and spending to your plan, you will be able to see if you kept to the plan. But it is a bit late to discover this if you have overspent and doing so has a significantly bad affect on your life. So, if it is critical to your future reward that you stay in control, you need some key triggers that will indicate that you may be slipping. (I am of course talking here about when you can overspend without the bank stopping your card or refusing cheques.)

> you need some key triggers that will indicate that you may be slipping

Take a look at your plan. In the section where you have a choice on how much you spend, or whether you spend at all, look at some of the spending that depends on how many times you do something. For instance, if you allow £50 for eating out or getting a takeaway, estimate how many takeaways or meals out that might be and keep track of that instead of the money.

brilliant example

When Rob and Andrew moved into their flat they did not want to cook for themselves every day. They agreed that they would set aside an amount of money every month for takeaways. They worked out that on average that would mean three takeaways a month or six trips to the burger bar. Rob was in charge of keeping count, which he did by keeping a magnet number on the fridge by the phone. Each time they ordered a takeaway, he changed the number. Three weeks into the month Andrew went to order another takeaway and was quickly reminded by the number on the fridge that they had already used up their allowance.

Rob and Andrew did not remove their ability to overspend. They just found an easy way to remind them that they had agreed a budget and if they ignored the sign they would overspend. It was still their decision at the end of the day. See if you can find similar ways to keep track of those items where spending can get out of control if you don't keep an eye on it.

brilliant recap

- There are five relevant principles to live by:
    1   Know your goal and use it to make decisions.
    2   Be bothered.
    3   File and organise your paper.
    4   Do not ignore bills.
    5   Use a calendar to plan.

- When making financial decisions, the first step is to write down your goal or reward. Organise the information into a table format showing the cost and the benefit. Choose the option that takes you towards your goal with either the greatest benefit or the least cost, depending on your need and resources.

- To give you a chance of being in control, make life and finances as simple as possible:
    - use direct debits and standing orders;
    - reduce the number of cards you carry;
    - use online banking;
    - make a list and deal with one thing at a time;
    - set limits and keep to them.

- Use a calendar or diary to collect financial information as you go about your daily life, to make planning less of a chore. Bring this information together in a monthly forecast at the end of the month; start with a three-month forecast and gradually build up the cash flow plan until you have a forecast covering the next 12 months.

- Review the actual spend each month with your forecast, seeing where you got it wrong or need to add some more control. (An online copy of the template is available at www.brilliantpersonalfinances.co.uk)

- Develop everyday habits that help to reduce the amount you have to think about – this will leave you free to focus more on getting your reward.

- Finally, find ways to keep track of whether or not you are keeping to your plan by linking your activity to what you spend. (For example, not taking lunch to work costs £6 each time; so how many times a month have you budgeted to buy lunch? Every trip to town costs £20 because you have to buy the children something to eat or a toy; how many trips have you budgeted for?)

CHAPTER 12

Pulling it all together with top tips

n this chapter you will find a summarised version of the information provided in the previous chapters. It is a chapter of
revision: a chance to remind you of some of the points
covered in the book.

Using Figure 12.1 on the next page, let's look at the simple
process to follow.

Finding the motivation and reward

The first part of the process involves finding a reason and reward
for making the effort to change the way you manage your
finances.

Use quiet moments of currently wasted time to work out what
you want from your life and finances. Ask yourself:

- What worries me about money?
- What can't I do right now?
- What does the future hold?

Use the answers to put a goal in place to get what you want and
change what you are unhappy with.

To get what you want, you need to know what it is and then
focus on getting it. You need to repeat the process of discovering
what you want from life, at least once a year – or more
frequently, if your goals are very short term. Use Tables 2.1, 2.2,

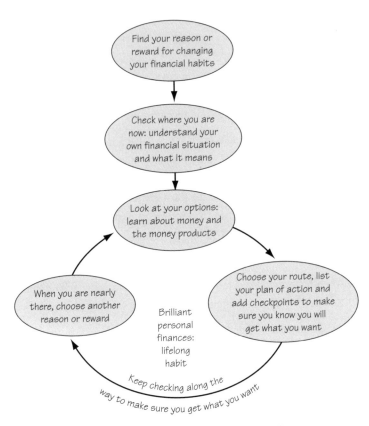

Find your reason or reward for changing your financial habits

Check where you are now: understand your own financial situation and what it means

Look at your options: learn about money and the money products

When you are nearly there, choose another reason or reward

Choose your route, list your plan of action and add checkpoints to make sure you know you will get what you want

Brilliant personal finances: lifelong habit

Keep checking along the way to make sure you get what you want

Figure 12.1 Brilliant personal finances: your personal journey

2.3 and 2.4 (copies are in the Appendix on pages 211–214) to help focus your thoughts. You can do this while on the train to work, having a cup of tea in the morning, after a session at the gym, soaking in the bath or while you are in the bathroom for some other reason! In fact you can do this exercise anywhere where you just have a few quiet minutes to yourself while you are waiting for something or someone.

Remember, money is a tool to be used to live your life. If necessary, remind yourself of the brilliant action from Chapter 2:

🔎 brilliant action

When you have worked out your short- and long-term rewards, write them down and put them where you can read them every day. You need to remind yourself why you are putting the effort in!

● Write them on a reasonable size piece of paper and put them preferably somewhere where you will see them the minute you wake up. One of my workshop attendees put them on the ceiling, as most people wouldn't see them there but she would see them every morning.

● If you use a computer regularly, have your reward written on your screensaver. Another workshop attendee told me he would put 'Life without debt' on his screensaver, as that was his aim.

● If the screensaver idea is too in-your-face or public, get your electronic calendar to send you a reminder every day.

● Use your partner, husband, wife, friends etc. to remind you every now and then of your reward so that you don't make the wrong decisions. A short text is sometimes all it takes.

● If you use a calendar (desktop or wall) write your reward on every page so that each time you turn to the next month you see it again for the first time.

☀ brilliant tips

Motivation and reward: reminders

● Being brilliant at personal finances requires action and commitment.

● Understanding personal finances and the most financially beneficial decision on its own does not make you brilliant at personal finances.

▶

- You need a reason, reward or at least negative motivation to make you take action.
- Use simple questions with *honest* answers to find the reward that matters.
- Generally there is one reason that is more important than the rest that will give you a reward for changing your habits and taking control.
- You should review your view of life, and how money affects it, at least once a year.
- You can review and plan anywhere that you have a few quiet minutes to yourself.
- Try to find a way to remind yourself of your goals every day.

Using your money personality

Understanding your money personality will help you to avoid pitfalls in decision making and will allow you to put a plan together to take more control of your finances without simply having to resort to willpower.

Remember that our emotions, past experiences, the media and other people's comments all affect our choices.

You could be:

- a big spender who cannot resist a purchase when out and about;
- a person who finds it hard to part with money;
- the one who always feels they have to pay;
- the one who finds it hard to take a risk;
- a big risk taker.

brilliant tips

Your money personality: reminders

- If you want to save for the future but can't resist retail therapy, then save before you get your money. Use a company saving scheme or set up a standing order for savings to come out of your bank account on pay day.

- Not spending money when you can afford to is reducing the pleasure of living. Find someone with the opposite personality to help you talk through the positive reasons for your spending decision. Ask yourself: 'Will I still be able to afford to meet my financial commitments and will this decision contribute towards achieving my goals?'

- If you are always over-generous, remember that it can affect your own future. Sometimes try not to be the first to offer to pay. When organising a group trip, get everyone to pay upfront for tickets. When out with a group for the night, suggest a kitty.

- Understand your attitude to financial risk. When planning investments, if you verge on the safe side then remember that you may not be able to go for the biggest return in the shortest time. You may need longer planning time to reach your goal. If you verge more towards the risky side, have a contingency in your plan in case it all goes wrong. Make sure you can manage if you take a gamble and then lose your investment.

Many of your current financial decisions and money management habits are dictated by your money personality. This personality may be based on early life experiences or just your make-up. For a balanced view and approach to money management and financial decision making, you need to understand and at times contradict your money personality. In order to achieve your goal, you may have to ignore the urge to spend on items that are not a necessity, or go against your frugal nature and spend savings on something that will meet a life goal for you, your partner or your family.

Understanding your finances

There are two sides to your finances: money coming in and money going out. We have focused primarily on controlling the money going out, since this book is about how to deal with money rather than how to make it.

The first step in taking control of your finances is to establish what you actually do with the money you have. Using Tables 4.1, 4.2, 4.3 and 4.4 (copies can be found in the Appendix on pages 215–218) you can record and analyse the last three months of your income and expenses to see where you need to, or can, take action. You will be surprised at how the small daily amounts add up.

The results will show that either you spend more than you earn, you balance the books, or you have surplus money left over. Whatever the result, it is your goal that will dictate whether or not you look for savings and a way to release more money to put towards attaining your reward.

In the tables your finances are split between fixed and discretionary spending. This allows you to focus on the area where you have some choice overspending and allows you to create more disposable income. You can then spend time reviewing your fixed expenses and your income to see if there are further opportunities to save or create income.

knowing what you do with your money gives you the power to make decisions

Remember, knowing what you actually do with your money gives you the power to make decisions that can change your life. Once you have found that you can balance your income and expenses, you can make choices about what to do with your money and possibly find that rewards you thought were out of reach are not so unattainable after all.

Understanding how financial institutions view you

Making decisions about managing your finances requires an understanding of the money products and how your current and previous financial behaviour affects your choices. Your current and previous financial behaviour is recorded by credit reference agencies (Equifax, Experian and Callcredit). They hold information collected from:

● local authorities;

● court registers;

● financial institutions;

● you or people financially associated with you.

The information they hold will tell potential lenders:

● how financially stable and reliable you are;

● how much credit you already have;

● how often you have applied for credit.

All this information is used to create a credit score.

brilliant tips

Your financial behaviour: reminders

● Being considered a low financial risk gets you the best deals and stretches your money further. To obtain credit at the lowest cost you must appear to be as stable and reliable as possible. If you are moving away from your home for a period of time but then returning, consider just redirecting mail to the new address rather than making it a permanent move.

▶

- Signing an application form often means you have agreed to legally binding terms and conditions.

- Develop the habit of asking 'Can you explain the small print?' before signing anything.

- If you are regularly being charged for late payments or for going above your agreed credit or overdraft limit, look at your statements for the last six months, add up all your charges and find something you could have bought or done with the money. This will give you a good reason for being more organised. Avoid late charges by setting up a direct debit for the minimum payment each month. You can always make an extra payment if you can afford to pay more than the minimum required.

- Bad payment history stays on your credit report for six years. Court judgments and bankruptcies stay until satisfied and clear.

- Use Table 5.3 (a copy is on page 220) as a tool to improve your credit score. Make a copy of the page and put it somewhere where you will look at it at least once a month. Start with the entries in the 12-month column; as you progress and the time without missing a payment on that particular agreement exceeds 12 months, then cross out your entry. Promise yourself a small reward for each crossed out entry. When you have crossed out all the 12-month column entries, throw the paper away and give yourself a final reward.

- The bad financial behaviour of your associates brings down your credit score. Before opening a joint account with someone for convenient bill payments, consider their financial behaviour. If it is not as reliable as yours, then split the bill payments equally between you instead. For example, one person will pay the gas bill and the other person will pay the electricity bill and so on. At the end of each month or quarter check to see there is a fair 50/50 split. Make sure that the bills you are each actually paying are in your respective names. This way, late payments only affect the credit report of the person whose name is on the bill.

- If you want to get rid of an old store or credit card you no longer use, and which has a zero outstanding balance but has a bad payment history, don't close the account until the missed payment history drops off your credit report. Also, contact the organisation and ask for your credit limit to be reduced to the lowest value possible. Work out when your bad payment history will disappear and put a note in your calendar or diary, or if you use an electronic reminder add this as a forward date, to remind you to cancel the card or account.

- When shopping around for the best deal, ask for a quotation rather than apply for credit. When the lender confirms that you can have the credit at the best deal, then you can finally apply. If the lender makes a quotation search, this does not leave a visible mark on your report for other lenders to see.

One other area that financial institutions are interested in is your net worth. This is the value of all your debts (the money you owe) taken away from the realistic value of all the things you own that could be sold and turned into cash. If you want to borrow money, then having a positive net worth can make you seem more attractive to the lender.

Reviewing your financial choices and understanding the money products

Once you have a list of all the items that make up your net worth, you can work through this list and review whether or not your current situation suits your needs and future goals. Remember: decisions affecting your financial situation should be taken within the context of your financial and life goals.

understanding how money products work allows you to make informed decisions

Understanding how money products work allows you to use expert advice to make informed decisions. To get the best from your finances it is important to understand the effect of compound interest. Compounding and regular saving can produce the lump sum you need for that future event. With compounding, you basically receive interest on the interest already given to you, so long as you leave it in your savings account. This allows you to make money from other people's money.

There are many bank accounts and savings accounts available and a basic list can be found in Chapter 7. Most accounts require a credit check but even people with bad credit history can still have a basic bank account where no credit check is required.

brilliant tips

Savings: reminders

- When deciding whether to save or borrow, take the total amount to be paid back from borrowing less the amount you would need to pay into a savings plan. This would be the extra cost of borrowing. Think about what you could do with that money if you did not have to pay it to the money lender.

- Try living on the current weekly state pension to see whether or not you need to plan for extra income when you retire.

- If you have been working and paying your national insurance in the UK, then every couple of years you should ask the Pension Service, part of the Department for Work and Pensions, for a forecast of the state pension you will receive when you retire. You can do this online at www.direct.gov.uk, under the heading

'Money Tax and Benefits'. This will give you a starting point to working out the extra income you may need when you retire.

- It is always cheaper to keep things regularly maintained rather than letting them run down and then having to pay for major repairs or redecoration.

- If you plan to keep a relatively large value of shares and reinvest your dividend payments for when you retire then find out if these shares can be wrapped in a pension plan. This way, you will accumulate a pension fund with some tax relief from the government. This will depend on your circumstances and whether or not the cost of setting up the pension is more than the tax saving.

- Compound interest with regular savings provides faster growth in your pot of money.

- Remember to make use of ISAs, which are tax-free savings plans.

- The earlier you plan for your pension, the cheaper it is to create a large pot of money for your retirement.

- Never extend your mortgage to create savings, as the interest paid on the mortgage will generally cost more than the return on your savings investment.

Most of us at some point in our lives will use a mortgage product to buy a property. A mortgage is just a large loan over a long period of time. Like any other purchase, you should look for the one that has the features and benefits to suit your needs. Your credit score will affect your ability to get the cheapest products, so before applying for a mortgage or any other borrowing understand what the requirements are and who will qualify so that you can do what you can to make yourself an ideal candidate.

In contrast, credit cards are meant for short-term borrowing, although they still work in much the same way as a loan. You borrow the money and pay interest on the amount you have borrowed.

Remember to use long-term borrowing for items that have a long life and short-term borrowing for items that have a shorter life. Using a 20-year mortgage to pay for a car is an expensive option. Using a credit card to pay for a house over 20 years is extremely expensive.

 **tips**

Debts: reminders

- The key to clearing your debts as fast as possible is to obtain the lowest interest rate you can and then to pay back the amount you borrowed as fast as you can.

- When you get a pay rise or have a financial windfall that was not expected – and before you spend it all on a one-off item – look at what the impact would be on your future if that money was put towards reducing the time you have to pay off a debt.

- If you are not sure if your endowment policy was mis-sold, then go to www.which.co.uk/advice/mis-sold-endowments-how-to-claim or contact your local Citizens Advice Bureau for more advice

- Withdrawing cash using a credit card means you start paying interest immediately!

- Imagine you have a credit card with an uncleared balance and you have a good payment history. Applying for a 0% balance transfer credit card can work for you if you follow this rule: once you have received the card, transfer the balance and cut up the card. *Never use it.* Set in place a standing order to pay a regular amount every month, clearing the balance by the time the 0% balance transfer period ends. Job done!

- Never sign anything you don't fully understand.

- If you find yourself unable to save for a regular tax bill, then set up a standing order to a savings account so that the money is removed from your regular account every month. If you really cannot stop yourself from dipping into the savings account then set up a direct debit with HMRC so that you pay a regular amount every month, in advance, towards the bill.

- The reward you get for having debt must be worth more than the cost of the debt.

- Offset accounts and all-in-one accounts allow you to have accessible money and reduce the cost of your mortgage.

- Over-paying on loans and mortgages can significantly reduce the cost and the term of the loan.

Always remember that debt costs money and is only really a bad thing if it is out of control and does not contribute towards your life goals.

Planning for the life you want

Even with all the information that is available on the internet, in the media and in books, it is generally impossible for the average person to become enough of an expert to make all their financial decisions without help. This is when a financial adviser is usually sought out. A financial adviser is an expert in money products.

Using an expert to help you make informed decisions is a smart move, but if your debt situation is out of control then do not go to a paid adviser – you need all of your money to pay off your debts.

When looking for a financial adviser, make sure they are suitably qualified for your needs by asking the following key questions:

- What qualifications do you have and what are you qualified to advise on?
- Are you independent or tied?
- What area of financial advice do you specialise in?
- How long have you been working in this area?
- How will you be paid?

It is important to be well prepared for the first meeting. You are paying for the advice and so you need to make sure it is relevant to your situation. Make sure that you:

- know what you want from your finances;
- bring with you your net worth and income and expense analysis;
- bring with you any relevant existing financial documents.

brilliant tips

Financial advice: reminders

- If you want to know about pensions, don't go to a mortgage adviser.
- Don't forget to tell your adviser something relevant; otherwise you may end up with the wrong advice.
- A financial adviser provides advice; the decisions, however, are yours.
- Never feel that you should be in a hurry to make a decision just because the adviser is impatient and pushing for an answer. Ask the adviser why a fast decision is needed. If they say it is because there is a time limit on the offer, ask them to show you the details and explain how much it will cost if you do not decide in time. Make sure you understand the decision deadlines and available cooling-off period so that you can change your mind if you need to.

When planning for your future reward, there are five relevant principles to live by:

1 Know your goal and use it to make decisions.

2 Be bothered.

3 File and organise your paper.

4 Do not ignore bills.

5 Use a calendar to plan.

When making financial decisions, the first step is to write down your goal or reward. Organise the information into a table format showing the cost and the benefit. Choose the option that takes you towards your goal with either the greatest benefit or the least cost, depending on your need and resources.

To give you a chance of being in control, make life and finances as simple as possible:

● Use direct debits and standing orders.

● Reduce the number of cards you carry.

● Use online banking.

● Make a list and deal with one thing at a time.

● Set limits and keep to them.

Use a calendar or diary to collect financial information as you go about your daily life, to make planning less of a chore. Bring this information together in a monthly forecast at the end of the month; start with a three-month forecast and gradually build up the plan until you have a forecast covering the next 12 months. Use the cash flow template in Tables 11.4, 11.5, 11.6 and 11.7 (copies are in the Appendix on pages 225–227); (an online copy of the template is available at www.brilliantpersonalfinances.co.uk).

Review the actual spend each month with your forecast, seeing where you got it wrong or need to add some more control.

Develop everyday habits that help to reduce the amount you have to think about – this will leave you free to focus more on getting your reward. And finally, find ways to keep track of whether or not you are keeping to your plan by linking your activity to what you spend.

brilliant tips

Financial planning: reminders

- If your personality means no matter how important something is you will probably forget to do it on time, then get someone else to do it. Get the company you need to pay to collect their payment by direct debit.

- If your debt situation means that you are considering bankruptcy or an individual voluntary arrangement, then talk to the credit card company and make them a payment offer to clear the debt. Ask them to freeze the interest and to accept a regular amount each month until the debt is cleared. If they think this is the best way to recover their money, they may agree.

- The free not-for-profit advice centres mentioned in Chapter 9 can help you to negotiate.

- You can still have a bargain in the sales without saving first, if you borrow and pay back wisely.

- Make your financial life as simple and straightforward as possible to give you more time and less stress.

Here is a reminder of everyday habits that will help:

- Use a fridge list: when you begin to run low of one item in the household then add it to the list.

- Put loyalty vouchers and discount vouchers straight in the bag, purse or wallet that you will have with you when you shop.

- If you manage your life on a timetable or diary, make an appointment with yourself to make your lists or look at your finances.

- If you don't know how you spend so much each day on sundry items, give yourself a limited amount of pocket money and leave the card at home.

- When it comes to throwing something away that is not broken, think about selling it in the local paper or on the internet.

- Get other people to remind you about regular jobs like servicing the car.

When you are close to reaching your goal

This all may seem like a daunting task but if you tackle it in small chunks you will be surprised how easy it is to bring the habits into your daily life. When you feel you are making progress towards achieving your goal, use the templates and questions in Chapter 2 to rethink where you would like to aim next. Always having a reward to look forward to will make you feel more inclined to think about how you manage your money. If you have a family, then choose a reward that everyone will benefit from, so that they will share the effort and work together.

All habits take time to form. You may not remember, but when you were a small child simple things such as how you talk, walk and eat were habits you had to learn. Now most of us take these for granted. Managing your finances in a controlled way is a habit you can learn – and one day it will become something you just do!

The last sections of the book contain blank copies of the tables mentioned in this chapter, plus all the definitions and more for your reference. Now it is up to you to continue in your quest to be *brilliant at personal finances*.

Appendix: Personal finance workshop materials

In this section you will find blank copies of tables introduced in the book (you can also find the templates at www.brilliantpersonalfinances.co.uk). Feel free to copy the tables, or fill them in here, as you go on your journey towards being brilliant with personal finances.

Table 1.1 Action list

Topic	Actions needed by me/us

Table 2.1 Motivation exercise: question 1

What worries me about money and my life?

Now

In the future

Table 2.2 Motivation exercise: question 2

What does my current money situation stop me doing/having?

Now

In the future

Table 2.3 Motivation exercise: question 3

When I think about money and the future, what do I see?

In one year

In five years

Table 2.4 Motivation exercise: question 4

When I think about money and the future, what do I want to see?

In one year

In five years

Table 4.1 Income

My income	Month 1	Month 2	Month 3
Salary 1			
Salary 2			
Freelance income 1			
Freelance income 2			
State benefits			
Pension			
Maintenance			
Child support			
Investment income			
Rental income			
Other			
Other			
TOTAL			

Table 4.2 Fixed spending

No choice: money out	Month 1	Month 2	Month 3
Utilities			
Rent and service			
Mortgage			
Insurances			
Communication			
Food			
Transport			
Medical			
Child-related			
Debt payments			
Finance charges			
Investments and savings			
One-off items			
TOTAL			

Table 4.3 Discretionary spending

Your choice: money out	Month 1	Month 2	Month 3
Eating and drinking			
Gambling and tobacco			
Household			
Subscriptions			
Activities			
Reading			
Music			
Travel			
Pets			
Grooming			
Occasions			
Clothes and accessories			
Investments and savings			
One-off items			
Other			
TOTAL			

Table 4.4 Spending habits

How to work it out	Summary	Month 1	Month 2	Month 3
A: Copy from Table 4.1 total	Total: money in			
B: Copy from Table 4.2 total	Total: fixed spending			
C: Take row B amount away from row A amount	Money left for discretionary spending			
D: Copy from Table 4.3 total	Total: discretionary spending			
E: Take row D amount away from row C amount	Money left over or overspent			

Table 5.1 Credit agreements

Credit card, store card, loan or finance agreement	Late payment penalty	Date next payment is due

Table 5.2 Proof of where you live

Address	Registered to vote from moving in	Can't prove I lived there

Table 5.3 Credit record

Credit agreements in last six years that you have not cancelled (loans, credit/store cards, mobile phone contract, rental and finance agreements for goods and services)	How long have you had the agreement?	Have you ever broken the agreement?	Number of times paid late in the past 12 months	Number of times paid three months late in the last six years
Peter's Barclaycard (credit card)	5 years	✓	1	5

That was not so bad, was it? Look at the table again. Have you missed anything?

Table 6.1 Net worth

Things owned by me/us	Amount	Things owed by me/us	Amount
Cash		Mortgage	
Bank accounts		Credit cards	
ISAs		Bank loans	
Endowment insurance/savings plan		Bank overdraft	
Pension plan		Store cards	
Property		Hire purchase	
Shares		Student loan	
Cars		Catalogue	
Jewellery		Friends and family	
Antiques/art/collectables		Unpaid tax	
Other equipment		Other bills	
Other		Other	
TOTAL 1		TOTAL 2	

My/our net worth (Total 1 minus Total 2) = £

Table 10.1 Action plan

Action category	By this date	I/we will have achieved	Through these actions
Be in control and stop wasting money			1 2 3 4
Reduce or clear debt			1 2 3 4
Save or borrow efficiently for a specific event or purchase			1 2 3 4
Plan for future income or retirement			1 2 3 4

Table 10.2 Potential cash

	Month 1	Month 2	Month 3
A: Money left over or overspent (from row E in Table 4.4)			
B: Less unnecessary spend			
C: Less extravagant spend			
D: Money left over or overspent			

Table 11.2 Spending options

What are you buying?	How will you plan to pay for it (i.e. savings, credit card, HP etc.)?	When will you get the item?	What is the set-up cost?	What will it cost per month?	What will be the total cost over the time to pay?

Table 11.3 Investment options

What is the investment?	What are you guaranteed to get?	How much will you pay in total?	What is the monthly investment?	When will your investment mature?

Table 11.4 Cash flow plan: income

Income	Month 1			Month 2			Month 3		
	Forecast	Actual	Difference	Forecast	Actual	Difference	Forecast	Actual	Difference
Salary									
Freelance income									
Benefits									
Pension									
Maintenance									
Child support									
Investment income									
Rental income									
F: Total income									

Table 11.5 Cash flow plan: expenses – fixed or no choice

Expenses: Fixed or no choice	Month 1			Month 2			Month 3		
	Forecast	Actual	Difference	Forecast	Actual	Difference	Forecast	Actual	Difference
A: subtotal fixed expenses									

Table 11.6 Cash flow plan: expenses – discretionary or your choice

Expenses: discretionary or your choice	Month 1			Month 2			Month 3		
	Forecast	Actual	Difference	Forecast	Actual	Difference	Forecast	Actual	Difference
B: subtotal discretionary expenses									

Table 11.7 Cash flow plan: expenses – unplanned and debts

Expenses: unplanned	Month 1			Month 2			Month 3		
	Forecast	Actual	Difference	Forecast	Actual	Difference	Forecast	Actual	Difference
C: Subtotal unplanned									
Additional debt payments									
D: Subtotal debt payments									
E: Total expenses (A + B + C + D = E)									
Over/underspend F minus E									

Brilliant jargon busting

AER Annual equivalent rate. Very similar to APR, but generally used for savings accounts.

APR Annual percentage rate. The interest you will pay on any money that you borrow if you do not pay the money back for one year. For example, imagine you borrow £100 from the bank or spend £100 on your credit card. The APR is quoted as 10%. You do not pay the money back for one year. You will then owe an extra £10 to the bank or credit card company in interest. The total amount owed will be £110.

ATM Automatic teller machine (often called 'hole in the wall').

Bank of England base rate The Bank of England will lend money to other banking institutions. Like all money lenders, it will want a reward for its trouble. It will charge interest at a set rate, which is reviewed every month.

Bonds A way of lending money to an organisation for a fixed amount of time and for a fixed payment of interest. It can be a low-risk investment.

Capital gains tax If you make a profit on any investment, the Government want to take some of it in tax. Everyone has an allowance that they can earn before the Government takes this tax. The allowance is given for each tax year, so if you are expecting to make a profit or gain more than your annual allowance, then it is worth seeing if you can split this across two tax years.

Cash card A plastic card that you can use to withdraw cash from the bank or ATM.

Cheque book A book of paper where you write the amount you want the bank to pay to the person whose name you have put at the top. The person you give the cheque to must give it to their bank, so that the bank can request the money to be transferred to that person's own account.

Credit reference agency An organisation that has a legal right to keep a record of the credit history, payment performance and related identity information of individuals. It makes this information available to anyone planning to offer credit to the individual, *provided they have permission and the right to see the information.*

Credit report A report prepared by credit reference agencies, with a summary of all the information they have been provided with or gather about you and your financial performance.

Credit score The number given to you by a credit agency or potential lender, based on information provided by you, other lenders and public offices such as the local authority council and courts of law. This score is used to rate how risky you are in terms of personal finance management.

Debit card A plastic card that you can use to pay for goods. The money is taken from your bank account immediately: it is a plastic form of cash.

Direct debit An instruction or order given by the bank or building society's account holder to the bank or building society to pay a particular organisation the amount they demand on an agreed regular basis.

Discounted variable interest rate mortgage Where the mortgage company agrees to reduce their standard variable rate by a specific percentage for a period of time. This means that if the organisation's variable rate goes up then your interest rate goes up, if their standard variable rate goes down then your interest rate goes down.

Dividends What you get if you buy shares in a company that is making profits. The company shares out the profit to all the shareholders once a quarter, twice a year or once a year.

Electoral register A list of all people who have registered and are eligible to vote in UK political elections. The register confirms their current address and that the voter is over 18.

Endowment insurance A type of life insurance. The insured person pays a monthly premium to the insurance company for an agreed length of time (typically 20–25 years). The insurance company invests the money paid to them, less their fee. At the end of the time period (the policy maturity date), the value of the life insurance is paid to the insured person (if they are still alive).

Equity Often used to mean a share in a company. It is also used to mean the amount of money tied up in a property: the difference between the value of the property and the amount owed on the mortgage.

Equity release plan A way of releasing the value of your property in cash without actually selling. It is a lifetime mortgage that you do not have to pay back in your lifetime: the money is paid back when you die and the property is sold. Interest is calculated every year and added to the amount you owe.

Extended warranties A form of insurance. You are often asked to pay for this insurance when buying something like a TV. The idea is that you pay something like £50 for the year and then if your TV breaks down you don't pay any extra to have it repaired.

Financial associate Someone with whom you have a financial link, such as a joint bank account or mortgage. Their details will be included in your credit report so that a lender can check their payment performance and use this as part of their analysis of your risk as a debtor.

FTSE (Footsie) Financial Times Stock Exchange. The organisation that produces the information relating to the performance of the top shares traded on the London Stock Exchange.

Guarantee card A card that goes with the cheque book. The person you give the cheque to can quote the number of your card and this will guarantee that the money is transferred from your account to theirs, even if you don't have enough money in your account. The card usually has a limit of £50 or £100.

Hire purchase inflation Also known as rent to buy: you rent the item until you make the last payment and then it belongs to you. It is usually only used for large value items. For example, imagine you want to buy a car for £20,000 but do not have the cash. A finance company buys the car on your behalf. You then make an agreement with them to make a number of hire payments to them with one last payment, at which point the car belongs to you. The hire payment will include an amount of interest that can be quite high and depends on the length of the agreement. It is possible to pay up to one and a half times the value of the purchase by the end of the agreement.

Interest-only mortgage A loan for a specific amount and period of time borrowed from a mortgage provider to buy a property. If the loan is not paid back at the end of the period, the mortgage provider can repossess the property in order to obtain the amount owed. Over the period agreed, the borrower pays an agreed amount of monthly interest but nothing towards paying back the amount borrowed; the full amount is then paid back at the end of the time period. The borrower effectively rents the money until it is time to pay it back.

ISA Individual savings account: a savings plan that meets criteria approved by the UK Government and allows you to have the profit without paying tax on it. You have a limit on the amount you can place in your ISA each tax year (the tax year runs from 6 April to 5 April the next year).

MIG Mortgage indemnity guarantee. Another type of insurance policy. It is generally required when you borrow more than 90% of the value of a property you are purchasing. The insurance protects the mortgage provider if you fail to make your mortgage payment. Not all mortgage providers require you to take out this insurance.

National Savings and Investments A range of savings and investment products provided by the Treasury and sold through the Post Office.

Net worth The value of all your debts (the money you owe) taken away from the realistic value of all the things you own that could be sold and turned into cash.

Options A complex investment product that is a little bit like gambling. Very simply, you buy the right to acquire shares at a set price in the future. You are gambling that the market price is higher than the option price you have bought, and that you can sell the shares straight away and make a profit. This is not to be attempted unless you understand the rules of the stock market.

Overdraft facility Where the bank lets you spend more than you have in your account. You will then be charged interest and possibly a fee for using their money.

PIN Personal identification number. A four-digit number that only you and the credit card company know. You will use this number to confirm you are allowed to use the card when buying something in person and processing your card through a machine. You will have agreed with the credit card company that you will not give this number to anyone or keep it written down.

Premium Bonds A bond offered by the Treasury. Every owner is placed into a monthly prize draw with a chance of winning £1 million pounds.

Protective registration This places a warning against your address so that anyone carrying out a credit search will ask for more proof of identification before giving credit or granting a loan. The company may call or write to you to confirm that you have actually applied for credit. They may ask that you present your passport or some other form of photo ID before the application is approved.

Register of Judgments, Orders and Fines Registry Trust Limited holds and provides information about court judgments held against a person for non-payment of a debt. This information is made available to the credit agencies for inclusion in their credit reports.

Repayment mortgage Where you borrow an amount of money to buy a property. Every month you pay back some of the borrowed amount and some of the interest payable. At the end of the agreed term the whole amount has been repaid.

Stamp duty A tax you pay on certain purchases, such as property or shares.

Standing order An instruction to the bank to make a specific payment to someone on a regular basis.

Stock market The place where buyers and sellers of company shares and commodities come together to trade.

Tracker funds A product where the money you invest follows the movement of a chosen index such as the FTSE 100 (the top 100 quoted shares on the London Stock Exchange).

Tracker interest rate mortgage Where the mortgage company agrees to charge a specific percentage rate above the Bank of England interest rate.

Unit trusts Lots of investments pooled together, to spread the risk of one investment not doing well.

Index

Items in **bold** denote a definition term.

 9780273721826
 9780273720799
 9780273712350
 9780273714842

 9780273726463
 9780273725114
 9780273721239
 9780273731788

 9780273732556
 9780273730910
 9780273734147
 9780273730286

**Whatever your level, we'll get you to the next one.
It's all about you. Get ready to shine!**